FETISH BLONDE

Credits:
FETISH BLONDE
John Gilmore
ISBN 1 871592 65 8
First published by
Creation Books, 1999
Copyright © John Gilmore 1999
All world rights reserved
Cover photograph:
Simon Starkwell
Design: Bradley Davis, PCP International
A Bondagebest Production

Holding the gun in my left hand, I stuck the barrel between my teeth and half-gagging on it, pressed the steel muzzle against the roof of my mouth. Without hesitation I slid my right thumb into the guard and pushed the trigger.

The hammer snapped but the shell didn't fire. I held my breath, unmoving for moments, tasting metal and oil and a sudden nausea. My heart started pounding against my ribs. Its loudness beat in my head as if knuckles were knocking on bone. I hadn't wanted any thought—any pause; no second thinking in the process of blowing my brains to the far side of the sun.

Pulling the barrel out of my mouth—a trail of spit spilling down on my neck, I shoved the bed pillows aside and sat up. Looking at the pistol and swearing to myself there'd been a bullet in the chamber, nausea swept over me, a sick heat like a thick, hot blanket. I could smell my own fear and I almost puked.

I knew there were five 9mm shells still in the clip in the old box but and I couldn't remember the sixth cartridge going into the slot.

Somewhat clear-headed, I yanked back the slide and a single brass-cased bullet ejected out against my stomach. It bounced and rolled between my legs. My hand was shaking as I picked it up and stared at the stubby lead head—a faceless crown on a brass torso, minus arms and legs. Instantaneous death, a little more than an inch in length. I could reload, stack the pillow on my head again and try a second time. The gun was in one hand, the bullet in the other, when the phone started ringing, the red light flickering like an inflamed eye. I reached over to the desk and grabbed the receiver. I could hear music and voices.

"What is it?" I asked.

She was breathing hard. "I'm coming back to your room," she said. "I'll see you in a very short while." I started to say no—don't come back up—seeing you tonight was enough—goodbye. She hung up before I said it.

I replaced the phone in the cradle and set the gun on the desk. I stood the slug alongside it and sank back into one of the pillows. I stared at the velvet, flower-papered ceiling—white dots sprinkling through rivers of dahlias. I tried not to move. Muscles and nerves in my legs were jumping.

Shooting myself had been an idea hanging as tight as a Siamese twin. Months before leaving the States for Paris, but I'd never stuck the gun in my mouth or pulled the trigger. A bullet in my heart was how it had been—the same as the cheesy protagonist in a cheap movie I'd written the year before. Holding a shaving mirror in one hand while pressing the muzzle into his solar plexus. I'd tried it—a dry run, and vaguely recalled taking the clip from the gun, but couldn't remember cocking it to jump a shell into the chamber.

I'd long since surrendered the plan of pulling the plug on pills. In fact, since that stomach pump episode six months earlier in a New York hospital, I'd kept myself just on the safe side of the line.

Now as I lay on the bed, my brain polka-dotted with white specks, I tried recalling the valium and ludes I'd swallowed that afternoon, chasing them with saki until Divi and I had emptied the bottle. Declining the downers, she'd said, "That combination can kill a person." I said yes, I'd heard that rumor, but was sure one could die from a rotten marriage as easily, and without the uncertainty of the pills. When she left I opened the Bombay gin.

Divi Duval née Daniele told me she was leaving her half-Latvian, ex-stand up comic turned French movie star husband, Claude. I knew what she was doing with me—rolling back the three years since that last movie in Paris.

With my eyes drifting from the murky flower walls to the wall-papered backs of doors, I heard the sounds of the street outside on rue des Belles Feuilles. I was smelling fish and bread and flowers and a sweet aroma—a perfume like rotting gardenias or the sap from a broken branch.

It was Divi.

I hadn't heard her sneak into the room. She was looking at the gun on the desk. Her eyes were like deep green pools. The pink angora brushed my cheek and her bracelets jingled. Her wet and soft lips whispered against my face. "What we're doing is crazy and dangerous, you know, and if Claude finds out he will kill me and no doubt try to kill you." My throat was dry and I didn't say anything. "Is that why you have the gun, Jake?"

I breathed in the smell of her skin. She was on the bed and I turned my face to hers. She bent over and put her mouth on mine. Her tongue slid between my lips and I could taste the saki beneath the brandy she'd been drinking. No hallucination. I wasn't dreaming, but had trouble breathing as though I was underwater. Something in my stomach and chest was churning and rolling. "I don't remember your leaving," I said. "I must've fallen asleep."

"You passed out, Jake. The door was open. How do you feel?" she asked. I said fine. She kissed me again, then pulled her face back. "Do you want to do it again—what we did, Jake?" I placed my hand on her breast. "I've been thinking all night about what we did earlier," she said. "I have not been able to think straight, Jake. They were talking business percentages and I was flashing on what we tried to do. I was so turned on I almost wet my pants..." She moved around, laying her face on my chest. Smelling her hair, I could feel her heart beating through her breast.

"I don't know how I feel," I said.

She put the tip of her tongue in my ear, then whispered excitedly. "I want to try it again, Jake. I'm desperate—" Her hand squeezed between her stomach and the bed, and she said, "I didn't wet my pants—I've been holding it."

"Holding it..." I said.

"*All* of it." She pressed my fingers into her crotch. "You said it was magic..." she said.

"I did?" I asked.

"Yes..." she purred. "You said it was a spiritual experience. Don't you remember saying that?" Her green eyes widened, moist and soft like the insides of grapes squeezed from their skins. "I've been holding it all night for you, Jake," she said.

"Don't tell me—" I said. "Don't say anything—don't speak."

"I won't say anything," she said, angling her hand into the waist of my pants. She held my cock and balls, her fingers wrapping around me. The heat of her touch stirred me straight up but my head wasn't hard. My heart wasn't hard. There was no *wanting*—only a numb kind of curiosity. The fire was in my brain and my pulse raced because she was placing the situation in front of us again. She wanted to do it and squeezed my cock—pulling as if stretching me. I felt pain. "I did it for you," she said. "I want to do it again—in the bathroom..."

I pushed her hand away but held her wrist. Sitting up, I massaged the slick brown skin of her arm, running my other hand to into the sleeve of her sweater. She stared at me with her mouth open almost stupidly. Her eyelids drooped but her desperate gaze stayed steady and unblinking. "Let's go into the bathroom," she said, "and I'll turn on the shower."

"Now...?" I said.

"Now," she said. "We'll get in the bathtub. Don't you want to do it again?"

I unbuttoned my shirt, smiling faintly as she took the waist of her pink sweater and pulled it over her head. She stared at her breasts thrust upwards in the white brassiere, swollen and moist in the shadows, the pale umber skin shining as though coated faintly with oil. Sucking in her breath, her ribs expanding—breasts climbing higher on her chest, I followed her into the bathroom like a sleepwalker.

The last of our clothing was shed on the short hike across the black and white tiles to the tub. Though Divi's body was heavier than three years before during that movie where she'd bared it all for the first time, her slightly swayed bare back was still an incredible piece of sculpture. Her buffoon husband, Claude, had never appreciated such beauty—or desperation. He was in many ways a kind of monkey, banging the lids of cans.

Divi opened the American style shower door and slid it back on the metal track. After she got in, she turned on the hot water in the tub and steam rose about her.

I stepped over the rim and into the shower, the water rising over my feet. She backed further down the tub and turned the water off. Reaching up, she placed her hands on the door frame, the muscles stretching and flexing beneath her wet skin. I felt instantly weak and light as a feather, as though with any breeze that stirred through the steam, I'd lift into the air.

Running my hands over her breasts and her hips, Divi moving her body, swaying her waist back and forth while her hips rolled slightly the opposite way, breasts undulated wetly beneath my hands.

My hands slid all over her and we stood like that for moments. "Now—now," she said, spreading her legs, "I've got to piss, Jake—" Her thighs muscles tensed beneath the bronze skin like cables. "I'm going to piss—" she said. Her left leg angled out further and rising on the toes of that foot, a glistening stream shot out of her and struck the porcelain. It splashed with force against the tub, against my legs and over my feet—warm and steaming. I reached between her legs and felt the wet heat rushing out of her.

"More! More!" I said.

Clenching her teeth, she rolled her body forward then back, and around again—turning her back to me, a gyrating motion as she gripped the shower frame. Thrusting her ass out, she spread her legs wider, bending the knees slightly. With a pained face, her jaw jutting and the lower teeth clenching up and outward from the upper teeth, she began to push, clenching her eyes. She grunted a breathy groan, took several quick, deep breaths and said, "I'm going to do it—" she said. "I'm going to shit!"

"You're going to shit—" I said.

She grunted again. "Oh, god—"

"Shit—" I said. "You're wonderful. I want you to shit—"

"I am," she said, groaning. "I'm going to shit—"

"I want to see it," I said.

I caressed and squeezed her ass and got down behind her on my knees. Licking her back and hips and her ass, I looked at her pink hole as it pushed from within like a slow-beating pulse, throbbing open—closing—uncertain—a strange bud. It sort of gathered—opening outward like a mouth as I spread the cheeks of her ass. She stretched her legs even further apart, bending the knees into more of crouching position, though coming up on her toes. The muscles in her calves and thighs tensed like chiselled bronze. My hands were on her legs as if trying to climb beneath her skin. She cried loud once, a kind of sob—a shriek that hit the tiles as her body shuddered and shook.

Hiding her nakedness, Divi quickly cinched herself into her clothes. "It feels like this situation between us is in our minds," she said. "We are reaching out of ourselves to make a fantasy come true. It wasn't the same on the last movie. You and I come close now but we are driven apart by the same thing that attracts us." She smiled slightly. "One pushes the other away the closer we get—"

Rain was hitting the window and the gray light was splattered with shadow. Standing before the narrow balcony, I was picturing my body sprawled on the wet black pavement; little French cars bumping across my limbs and head as if lurching over lumps of concrete. I didn't say anything.

"It is an identity," Divi was saying, "like how you were in the movie long ago when you played a young Nazi gestapo. You were marvelous in that picture, Jake. It must have been the easiest role you ever played before you became a writer."

Her eyes averted from my back to the television. They were talking about Disneyland on the outskirts of Paris. She sat in the chair to put on her shoes. "You do not look well, Jake..."

"I'm becoming sick," I said.

"With me?" she asked. "Is that what you are saying?"

"No," I said. "Not because of this fling we're having again or what we're doing. It's just me."

"You were always sick," she said. "It's part of what makes you irresistibly attractive."

"Perhaps there's something passively attractive," I said, "but hardly irresistible."

"Possibly it is that you are *not* so attractive," she said, staring at me. "But are irresistible, Jake. It is the fascist in your nature. The cold and distant attitude you have."

"It has grown on me," I said. "Like a fungus."

"You were the same three years ago when we met. The same as you are now."

"You shouldn't leave Claude," I said. "You're well-matched with a fool like Claude."

"It's the reason I am here tonight—because I am a fool. Like I have been these few nights this month..." She got up, crossed the room and sat on the floor, placing her hand on my leg. "He does not know that I am leaving him," she said, massaging into my crotch. "But with you it does not matter whether I stay or whether I leave... It does not matter to you, does it, Jake?"

I stared at her. "You are detached from me," she said. "It is good..." She stroked my crotch, looked up into my face and said, "I want to suck your cock right now..."

The white dots disappeared in the daylight. After Divi left, I dressed carefully in a white shirt and tie, charcoal slacks and put on the blue blazer. Gathering my raincoat, I left the room and walked downstairs for juice, a croissant and coffee. Two chunky Germans wedged onto the delicate iron chairs were scrutinizing the midday menu. One kept looking over at me through slits of eyes like knife cuts in a head of cabbage.

I couldn't eat the croissant but gulped the coffee, burning my throat. The German smiled. Putting on my raincoat as I crossed the lobby, I didn't heard the girl's skate blades sliding on the marble floor. She bumped into me from the side, knocked off her sunglasses and cried, "My *god*! You are not looking where you are going—"

"Excuse me!" I said. "You're probably absolutely right—" Neither of us had toppled, I said, no harm done, and I picked up her yellow sunglasses. Snatching them, she then swept past, gathering the same momentum that'd almost knocked us over. But she came to an abrupt halt stop at the lobby doors, spun around with one foot at an angle and stared at me.

"Wait!" she said. Her eyes were wide and an almost yellow color in the irises with threads of pale green going around the edges. "It is *I* who am *sorry*!" she said. "How very clumsy of me— I am sorry, Monsieur Morgan!" The high black socks to her knees accented the slim bare thighs and a golden sheen to the skin sliding up into the green satin shorts. Tight as flesh and very low-waisted, showing her stomach and a silver ring pierced through the skin around her belly button. Some military patches decorated the sleeveless shirt hanging loose on her shoulders, but with the front tails tied high on her lower ribs.

One of her hands lifted as in greeting but the distance between us was too far for a shake. "Do I know you?" I asked.

The ends of her fingers stuck out of the black gloves, the leather digits cut at the middle joints. She had black lacquer on her bitten-down nails, and wore a Japanese headband above her brows— some kamikaze medal pinned in the center.

"I should know who you are—" she said, almost panting, "and not crash into the man who is writing the movie!" Her teeth were small and very white like an animal's. "We have never talked to each other," she said, "but I have seen you because I am working in *Sucant le Sang*!"

I stared at her. "Of course," I said. "You're the punk rocker the vampire's chasing..."

She nodded, beaming. "I am in the little boat on the Seine," she said, weaving on her skates. "The virgin in pink panties who is attacked by the awful vampire!" She made a fearsome look and growled comically. "You are writing the film for the godfather—"

Wide-eyed but joking, she feigned catching herself and slapped a gloved palm across her mouth. "I should not say such things about the producer!"

"I'm sure he doesn't mind," I said. "He's been rather proud of that tag since the success of our gangster movie with Claude Duval."

"Oh, *yes*," the girl said. "Monsieur Duval is a *wonder*ful vampire." She pulled down the front of the green shorts to show the bikini waistband of the pink panties she wore. "You see? I am wearing the pink panties!" Fine faint blonde fuzz on her belly reflected in the light.

Staring at her skin, I said, "Yes, I see... So did you enjoy working with him in the catacombs?"

"Oh, no–" she said, "I mean Claude Duval was not in the catacombs yet. They filmed me by myself, monsieur, running away from the vampire. That is before he catches up with me and *strikes* on the little boat."

"You're right," I said. "I wasn't on the set for the catacombs. The schedule's been changed somewhat–"

"Monsieur Duval will be chasing me in the sewers maybe the first of next week," she said. "I do not know what day. Robert Kamp tells me what days I will work. He says there is some problems with the arrangements–"

"Yes, we've experienced some unexpected delays," I said. "It's made a jumble of things."

"I think next week they are shooting the sewer scene," she said. "But the vampire does not get to bite me because I get away in the catacombs. Have you been in the catacombs, Monsieur Morgan?"

"Yes," I said. "I wrote them into the script, the same with the sewers."

"Ah, sometimes the sewers smell very bad," she said, "but I enjoy the catacombs because the skeletons of millions of dead people do not smell anymore. It is like the submarine movie when you were also an actor–where the submarine *blows* up and everybody burns so the bones are under the water and nobody can smell the dead."

"The submarine..." I said, and laughed. "You've actually seen that picture?"

"Robert—who is Monsieur Leefeldt's assistant—"

"I know—" I said.

"We watched a video of the movie on his television," she said. "He lives on the third floor here at the end of the hotel and his window looks at the Eiffel Tour." I nodded. She said, "He is not in his room now because I have just come from there. We are friends, and it was Robert who said, 'Oh, you must see the movie that Jake *Mor*gan made when he was a young actor.' We were on the set and the vampire Claude Duval said, 'Oh, yes, Robert, Jake Morgan was a *wonderful* actor.' So Robert said we must watch the submarine movie."

"I'm flattered," I said. "Was it subtitled?"

"Oh, yes, it has the French subtitles," she said. "I think Robert is very impressed because you are a famous Hollywood writer, Monsieur Morgan." Slightly edgy, she motioned toward the desk. "If David the clerk comes back he will get mad because I am skating on the floor again. I am always skating and he gets mad. He says 'You do not belong here!' But I say yes I *do* belong because I am a visiting Robert who is helping me. I am skating in a cotton underwear commercial because of Robert." She spun around in a swift, tight circle, the light hitting the fine blonde hair on her slim thighs. She spread her arms. "I am very good at skating."

"I can see that," I said.

"Also I am in another movie," she said. "Not a big one like *Sucant le Sang*, because it is only a video. But I am the *star* of it, so I must hurry! They are waiting for me."

"Who are 'they'?" I asked.

"The film students from the Institute who are shooting at the Arc de Triomphe and all over the Champs Elysée today!" She smiled again, lifting her hands, palms up, the small, black-nailed fingers protruding from the gloves. "So I must say goodbye for now. Are you taking a taxi past the Arc, monsieur?"

"I'm going the opposite way," I said, "for an interview with *Paris Confidential*."

"Oh, they are *very* nasty people," she said.

"They're taping it this afternoon and it's airing tonight," I said. "It's supposed to be live but it isn't."

"So is the man—the host Jacques Cardiff, supposed to be alive but I don't think he is—" She laughed, and said, "Maybe I will not miss it if I can see it on Robert's television." I was staring at the rise of her small breasts from the center of her ribs into the half-unbuttoned shirt. Some sort of chain, like a dog's leash hung around her neck and into the shirt. Looking at me carefully, she pulled the chain out and wagged a kind of Iron Cross medallion. "I am wearing this in the video!" she said, skating around in another quick, wider circle in front of me. Her yellow eyes seemed to glow and she had a perplexing little smile. "Now I must go," she said. "I look forward to saying hello to you again, Monsieur Morgan. Maybe we will meet on the set."

"You're in the boat sequence day after tomorrow," I said. "Perhaps I'll see you by the river."

"No..." She was shaking her head. "That will be Saturday very early in the morning. That is when they are filming that scene. I must go—" Spinning around, she burst ahead out the lobby doors, her green shorts reflecting a flash of light off the glass. Her rollerblades slid across the wet sidewalk with a dull, swishing noise, leaving two long tracks in the thin rain water.

I caught the door swinging closed, pushed it open and stepped out onto rue de Longchamp. The blade tracks curved around the corner but the girl had disappeared.

My hands were numb during the taping *Paris Confidential*, and slow pain hung in my chest as if by hooks. The thin host Jacques Cardiff, sat perched at the sound stage table like a crow eyeing a kill. His glance rarely met mine and the girl had been right—he had an embalmed look, except for his thin mustache which wiggled slightly above his pinched lips.

"So being a highest paid script 'doctor'," he was saying, "appears to have given you a King Midas touch in the exploitation field—"

I said, "If you mean I stuff turnips into gold-plated banquet jackets, I guess you're right."

"*Sucant le Sang* is hardly a *turn*ip, and from what I hear, Jake, it's blossoming into an extravaganza for Matthew Leefeldt's Triangle Films and his Japanese co-producers due to the notoriety the production has been stirring up."

"I wouldn't say 'blossoming'," I said. "The film's progress was determined before the shooting began, and yes, a chunk of the financing is out of Japan based on the success of Leefeldt's gangster film—"

"Which you wrote here in Paris three years ago," Cardiff said. "Isn't it true the Japanese financing for *Sucant le Sang* is pretty much based on the success of *other* motion pictures *you* have developed? According to Hiromi Nakasha, you're a regular moneymaking mastermind."

"That's a little far-fetched," I said.

He laughed. "You're too modest, Jake. There's the American tractor-horror movie you wrote that even out-grossed the Japanese in *Tokyo*! Not to mention the one with that 'three-stooges' serial killer running around the Louisiana swamps—"

"*Cajun Cut-up*," I said.

"What is Triangle Films?" he asked, "and how does this vampire movie now in production fit in?"

"The vampire movie is co-produced with Matthew Leefeldt under Triangle Productions—which is the British backing for the French film, with Leefeldt's end half-financed by the Japanese. It's not an unusual arrangement," I said. "But the vampire movie started out as a quick exploitation film Mark Lajos and I were developing for Allied in Hollywood, under a directing commitment Mark had with Allied. It wasn't even a *vampire* back then. We had a science-fiction desert-rat sort of zombie idea we were planning to shoot in Death Valley."

"It has certainly gathered airs since its transformation into a higher budget, French 'cult' film," Cardiff said. He was smirking and the small flecks of foam that had collected at the corners of his mouth spattered onto the table.

"The vampire was Matthew Leefeldt's idea," I explained. "He'd wanted to make a vampire movie for years, using the catacombs and sewers. He'd been inspired by that 1935 Charlie Chan movie, *Chan in Paris*, and the line in there where Chan says 'Many strange crimes have been committed in the sewers of Paris...'"

"Your wife—Ann Michaels," Cardiff said, "or is she now one of your *ex*-wives?"

"We're divorced," I said.

"Ann was to play the lead in the original zombie version—"

"No," I said. "That's incorrect. She wasn't signed by Allied and that piece of misinformation has caused a lot of problems all along—"

"To put it *mildly*!" Cardiff threw in. "Why does Ann Michaels insist she was supposed to play the lead in that movie?"

"Self-envisioned casting on her part," I said. "A day dream that hasn't an ounce of paperwork to back her claim. Ann and Mark had talked about her working in the picture, though I was against her playing the lead. It was nothing more than talk. When the additional financing sought by Allied was offered from London, the British also had a star of their own in the deal."

"Lovely Marjorie Lee,"Cardiff said. "And then, as they say—the trouble hit the fan."

"Not exactly how they *say* it," I said, "but that's what happened when Mark Lajos ran into some problems—"

"To say the least," Cardiff said. "And the 'notoriety' we mentioned is due—in part—to these same problems which I'd like to explore a little—"

"I'm at liberty to discuss only what's basically public knowledge," I said.

"Such as the alleged rape of your own thirteen year old step-daughter," he said. "Ann Michaels' child by a prior marriage—"

"Yes, to Burt Raymond."

"Another major movie star—"

"—of fading importance," I added.

"We *love* Burt in Paris," Cardiff said with a foppish grin. "He's the American version of our Claude Duval." I didn't respond. "So we have Mark Lajos accused of raping Ann Michaels' and Burt Raymond's biological daughter, a child of thirteen—"

"She's fourteen now," I said. "That's over a year ago."

"But the charge," Cardiff said, "is *rape*—and still *is*, I presume?"

"It's still an open charge," I said.

"And this accusation undermined the movie deal with Allied?" Cardiff said.

"It killed it," I said, "when Mark want to jail." Cardiff said something else but I lost it behind the memory of that shriek that'd cut through my head like a bullet into a sheet of metal. It wasn't my step-daughter's scream as she supposedly was being raped by Lajos, but of Ann finding the girl in the pool house with him, breasts bared, the bikini top soaking the chlorine on the boards. And the Hungarian filmmaker supposedly stuffing his pecker back into his pants.

My wife'd screamed "*Rape!*" into the Beverly Hills sunset and two cop cars hit the driveway as though laying in ambush. Wrestling the girl out of the poolhouse, Ann tugged the kid's bathing suit bottom up and down as they ran to the house.

From inside, all *I* saw was actor Nick Morris tipping his nose up from a line of coke and saying, "What the fuck's *happen*ing...?" Everyone's eyes popped over the half-naked kid as Ann rushed her into the kitchen and through the house, screaming, "My daughter's been *raped* by Mark!"

"The kid was *grinning* at me," Nick would later confide, "and her old lady couldn't see it—so busy yelling for the cops to arrest Mark!"

The police searched promptly but couldn't find the suspect who'd scampered around the pool (Nick'd later say "running like a thief—"), over the slope of ice plants and tried to get to his car, but the cops had parked behind him. Instead of running, he hid under Ann's convertible, having lost a shoe in flight.

It took a couple minutes for Mark to be dragged out from under the car, one of the most pathetic scenes I'd seen, topped only by Ann's wringing out the most anguished performance I'd ever seen her play.

The cops had a weeping Mark cuffed into the rear of a squad car while a lawyer named Beech—someone I'd never met—sprung onto the scene as though he'd been hiding in the bushes. He took charge of barricading the kid in her bedroom to be checked out by a lady doctor I'd never seen before either, and a Beverly Hills policewoman. Ann was looking at me as though seeing a cigar store Indian.

"I have to talk to my step-daughter," I told the lawyer. "My wife's making serious allegations and if the kid's been abused—"

He cut me off by slapping some papers into my hand. "The child can't be questioned at this time and certainly not by you."

"What are you talking about?" I said. "She's *my* step daughter—"

"She's Ann *Michaels'* daughter!" he said. "If you'll take a moment to read what's just served upon you, you'll see you're restrained from bothering the child or interfering with Ann—"

"*Bothering* the child?" I said, glaring at him.

"I'll fill in the blanks," he said. "It's very possible you will be named in a second complaint in this situation."

"What 'complaint'?" I said.

"A complaint of sexual molestation," he said.

"Me?" I said. "This is incredible! This is fantastic—"

"However you choose to interpret it, Mr. Morgan, I'd suggest you consult your attorney immediately, but first—the preferable action is for you to remove yourself temporarily and peaceably from the premises—"

"This is my house," I said.

"That might be an arguable point—" he snapped and turned to the tall policeman blocking the kid's bedroom door. The cop nodded, looked at me with a smile and stepped forward.

He said, "I sure like your Porsche, Mr. Morgan. Saw it the

minute we got here. That's a beauty." Placing a hand gently on my shoulder, he said, "Why don't we take a walk outside and get a better look at it?"

Grasping the situation, I let the cop escort me out of the house. In the driveway, I asked, "Am I under arrest? Is that what's happening here?"

"Oh, no, sir, " he said. "It's nothing like that." Then he said, "I'd like to tell you, sir, I think that movie of yours is right up there with *Friday the 13th* and the *Texas Chainsaw Massacre.*"

"Which one's that?" I asked.

"That redneck tractor killer picture," he said. "I've watched it a couple dozen times, Mr. Morgan. Whenever we'd go to the video store it'd be checked out, so I finally copied it off the tube." We were at my car and he asked, "How come you don't write any more movies like that one?"

"I do," I said. "I'm rewriting other people's mistakes right now—"

He shook his head a little and said, "That tractor movie's one of my favorites of all time."

"What about *Cajun Cut-up?*" I asked.

"That's a terrific one, too, sir," he said, "but mostly I like the tractor movie due to the way the police are handled in it. I mean, you've got it just the way it really is, without all the phoney stuff."

Thanks," I said, and stopped. "Look—why am I being removed from my own house?"

"I wouldn't say 'removed'," he said. "More of a recommendation until these legal things are sorted out by your lawyers."

"But what's happening with Mark Lajos?" I asked.

"Your wife's accused him of raping your daughter, so he's been placed under arrest for the time being." He put a firm hand on my arm, gently urging me to the car. "On the surface," he said, "it appears your daughter's—"

"My *step*-daughter," I said.

"Your step-daughter's been raped or sexually abused according to what your wife is saying she witnessed—"

"But how did this restraining order against *me* suddenly get into all this?" I asked. "I mean, this doctor—this lawyer—all of this like a rabbit popping up out of a hat!"

The cop said, "I can only tell you we received a call from the lawyer on behalf of your wife—"

"But he wasn't even *here*—" I said.

The cop shook his head again. Still with a smile, he said, "That's all the legal side of it, sir. We just carry it out and do our job like you showed in the tractor movie. Then it gets all worked out in court. Why don't you start your car up, Mr. Morgan? I had a 924 Porsche which they called a 'poor man's Porsche.' So the sound of your's will be like music to my ears..."

"But I've been drinking all afternoon," I said, looking at his name plate. "Is Oliver your first name?"

"That's my last name, sir."

I said, "So what happens, Oliver, if I'm too loaded to drive and I wreck the hell out of a bunch of automobiles?"

"Well," he said. "That could be a serious problem for you, sir..." He opened the Porsche door and helped me climb in, then shut the door and bent down, putting his face in the window. "Drive carefully, Mr. Morgan. I'd *person*ally hate to see you get in any other trouble over all this mix up."

Half-drunk, I turned the key and in seconds was speeding south to Sunset Boulevard. I jumped the signal accelerating into traffic, and thought how quickly one could die in a wreck. I pushed down on the gas, giving birth to the first thoughts of killing myself in some mangling collision.

But what if I didn't die instantly—what if there was pain or paralysis? I pictured Ann grinning at the foot of a cripple's bed with her bright eyes as empty as the inside of a new garbage can. I flashed on the hero of an unpublished novel I'd written back when I thought of writing something serious. A purposeless geek shuffling his way through an insurance firm, a rotten marriage, hateful kids and two mortgages. One day at a Hollywood intersection, instead of going home to shoot the wife and kids and himself, he turns left instead of right and keeps driving until he runs out of gas. He abandons his car on a desert side road and walks through the cactus until his shoes wear out—

Without thought, my foot hit the brake when another car zipped out in front of me. With a shakiness in my stomach, I eased on the gas and fell behind two slower moving cars. I saw Bob Hope in the rear of one car, but closer I noticed it was a cardboard placard of Hope.

I rolled north into the Beverly Hills Hotel driveway, parked facing a clump of palms and felt the front spoiler mash against the curbing. Destruction was setting in. I needed a drink.

After a gin and tonic in the Polo Lounge, I called my own lawyer, Bob Sherman, and clued him to the papers Beech'd pushed into my face. In an unconvincing tone, Sherman said he was shocked but not surprised. I said 'How come?' He said, "We'll talk." He'd make some calls and meet me in an hour. "Don't go back to the house," he warned. "They could arrest you, Jake."

Walking back to the bar I realized I'd slipped my feet into loafers but wasn't wearing socks. I ordered a second gin—a double, sipped it listening to the piped-in Honolulu melodies, and remembering the surfing movies and that quarter-million I'd plunked into the house when Ann and I married. I'd spent near an equal amount on Ann's shrink and her Prozac paradise, along with her kid's special school for the behavior disordered.

Sherman showed up, his cheeks red, flushed and saying he had a fever. "The Hong Kong bug," he said, then told me Ann'd recently ragged to him about suing Mark, Allied, and probably me for cutting her out of the zombie movie. I told him the same story: nobody'd signed her and whether or not she'd had the lead would've been Allied's decision. Sherman knew all that.

"I'm *your* attorney," he said. "I was on your side before you married her. I've handled your contracts and real estate, Jake, but she's got a fucking shark in Beech and they're out for blood."

"She screams," I said, recounting the day, "the cops rush in like out of Keystone reel, grab Mark, and then this lawyer's suddenly kicking me out of the house. I'm asking where it all came from so fucking *fast*?"

"I've sensed Ann's been planning something," he said, "but I hadn't anticipated a sneak attack. I couldn't believe she'd go this far. Mark's charged with statutory rape, Jake, I mean we're talking big time—assault, sexual abuse. Whatever else they're cooking up. I'm saying he's *nailed*. Now what do you know about this? Is any of this true?"

I had to say I didn't know. Maybe it could've been true. "Maybe it's Ann's knife in *my* back," I said. "Maybe that's what it is."

Sherman suggested I spend the night at the hotel. "I'll get to the bottom of this and call you first thing in the morning."

Only once before had I spent a night at the Beverly Hills Hotel, and that was when I'd passed out in the bungalow Leefeldt'd occupied while setting the gangster flick.

After a couple more drinks to kill the thirst, I lost track of what I was doing. I couldn't remember leaving the Polo Lounge or getting the room, or where the red haired girl came from or how long she'd stayed in bed with me. The next morning the plate of brown smudge and crumbs reminded me of room service and the chocolate cake coming in. The girl'd ordered cake. I remembered that.

I had my head under the faucet when Sherman's call came through. He said, "It doesn't look so good, Jake."

Sitting on the bed, water dripping from me, I asked him what he meant. A pair of blue panties were on the floor by my loafer. Vaguely I wondered who the girl had been and where she'd gone.

In a dry crisp voice, Sherman said, "Jake, I've *got* to ask if you've have ever had any physical contact with the kid?"

"What do you mean 'physical' contact?" I said.

"I mean 'physical *con*tact', Jake. Do you know of any occasion last year where you'd been alone with the girl and had some contact with her physically—like touching her privates?"

"Wait a minute," I said. "Bob, are you asking me if I've had sexual *contact* with the kid?"

"That's exactly what I'm asking, Jake."

I said, "Well, the answer's an overwhelming *no*! That's the most ridiculous question you've ever asked me. Where in hell did you get *that* idea?"

"The information came from your step-daughter," Sherman said. "According to Beech, the order's to keep you away from the child without exactly highlighting the reason." Even Sherman's voice sounded different—someone you've talked to a thousand times and suddenly there's someone else there. "They've got a statement from the girl, Jake, saying you've been alone with her and she's claiming you touched her privates. There's some question as to whether this happened more than once—"

"She's *lying*!" I yelled. "She's so dumb or spaced-out she wouldn't remember it anyway—"

"Remember *what*?" he asked.

"Whatever it is she's making up!" I said. "I'm using a figure of speech, Bob, to point out they're taken advantage of the kid to get her coughing up some stupid lie—"

"Being that as it may," he said, "you're sitting square on a powder keg, Jake, and this kid's holding the fuse. But they're giving us a break, and the charge the kid's made isn't being acted upon for the moment, you understand. It's what we call a suspension while Ann's filed for divorce—"

"Di*vorce*?" I said. "Jesus! When did all this happen?"

"I received papers this morning," he said.

"Okay," I said. "You won't get a gripe out of me on the divorce—"

"Better hold off on that until you see the bottom-line." I didn't say anything. He said, "Until we're final on the divorce settlement, the sexual misconduct charge made by the girl isn't going to be acted upon as long as we play ball."

"Play ball," I said. "What's the fuck's that mean?"

"It means pending the outcome of the settlement," he said.

"The *settle*ment," I said. "You're saying we sign on the dotted line—agree to whatever she's asking. What're we handing over anyway?"

"Well—the house and just about everything, Jake—"

"It's goddamn blackmail!" I cried.

Sherman was silent for a moment, then said, "I'm afraid so,

Jake. Either way—"

"What do you mean 'either way'?" I said.

"You'd no doubt be wiped out financially defending against the sex abuse charges if they're filed and you're arrested and have to stand trial. I can handle the divorce, Jake, but if we're going to contest it and force them to file these charges, I'm afraid we'll have to bring in some counsel experienced in sex abuse. Assuming they'll limit the charges to that."

"*Limit* them?" I said. "How can this *happen*?"

"Considering the complaints against Mark," he said, "I'd say they're in for a blue ribbon day. It would be your denial against the girl's testimony and with Mark's arrest—well, I'm saying they've built an impressive pattern—"

I cut him off. "I can't believe what you're saying to me. Ann's got some revenge scam going—"

"Again, be that as it may," he said, "it looks like Mark could hit the shit hole pretty hard, Jake, and it's very possibly he can take you right down with him."

Jacques Cardiff's eyes were boring into me as if drawing a bead down the sight of a gun. "—and while waiting to go to trial on the rape charges," he was saying, "Mark Lajos abruptly fled the United States os*tens*ibly to make a film in Paris."

I nodded. "That's partly correct," I said. "When Allied dropped the picture, Mark hooked up with the British team who bought the project to Matthew Leefeldt."

"But in order to *do* so," Cardiff said, "Lajos skipped out on his bail, illegally fleeing the country to avoid prosecution."

"That's public knowledge," I said.

"And he cannot return to your country," Cardiff said, "without being arrested as he steps off the plane."

"In all probability," I said.

"So enter Jake Morgan to the rescue!" Cardiff said. "You are now working *with* Lajos in Paris and for the British *and* the Japanese."

"Well, for Triangle Productions," I said. "Matthew Leefeldt

went for the project with the condition that I developed the script. He'd already involved the Japanese in a vampire idea with Claude Duval as an updated Dracula—"

"Duval starred in the gangster movie," Cardiff said, "which *you* wrote, Jake, three years ago when you married Ann Michaels on the Eiffel Tour!"

"Ann and I had been close for a year in Hollywood before the gangster movie."

Smirking again, Cardiff said, "During the making of that film, *Paris Match* ran an article about you and actress Divi Daniele—"

"Divi was working in the picture and we became friendly," I said.

"You *are* a master at understatement, Jake. They quoted you as saying you'd met Divi while scripting Leefeldt's gangster movie, to star Claude Duval and Ann *Michaels*, and that it was possible you wouldn't *marry* Ann because of your whirlwind involvement with Divi."

"That's not true," I said. "Divi and I—we became close for a short time during a brief period of misunderstanding between Ann and myself. My friendship with Divi basically faded after the film."

"You married Ann and returned to the States, and Divi Daniele married Claude Du*val* who now has the lead in *Sucant le Sang*—not opposite Ann Michaels but the beautiful Marjorie Lee—"

"That's right," I said.

"Which you have written and which Lajos is directing while seeking sanctuary in France!"

"We all get along famously," I said.

"*Very* well put, Jake Morgan. I do want to mention the next project which will be taking you to Japan."

"Yes," I said. "The script is based on a true case about a Japanese artist convicted of murder—"

"—who is a cannibal!" Cardiff said. "He *eats* the body of his young Caucasian victim and then becomes—" Cardiff's foam was gathering again, "—are we ready for it? He's sent to an insane asylum from which he is too soon released to become a gourmet critic on a *French tele*vision show!"

A pink-haired prostitute with freckles and orange lashes stepped out of a door north of the Champs, her red lips pulling at the ends as if by wires. Another girl appeared behind her, grinning and myopic-eyed. She poked her streaked and spiked high black hair, swaying from her crown like a mast of porcupine quills.

The rapidly fading sunlight still sparkled on the wet sidewalk, and the reflections shattered under my steps as I walked to Le President Cafe. I took the usual window table, ordered wine, a half plate of snails, and bread and mustard.

I tried to eat but the food hung between my mouth and throat. Fearing I'd choke if I swallowed what I'd chewed, I drank instead and scribbled notes on the back of an envelope.

I'd finished half a bottle and a waiter was removing the plate when I looked up to catch a yellow streak sweeping past the glass. It was the blonde girl on her rollerblades. She made a sharp sort of figure eight and came to a stop laughing in front of the window.

I was about to rap on the glass with the knife when a tall young man with thick black hair came hurrying behind her with a wheelchair in which another young man sat with his eye to a video camera, filming the girl. She threw out her arms against the cafe window, pressing herself to the glass—her palms flat on the pane, her thighs and breasts pushing until the glass seemed to bow in slightly. I could almost see the pores in the skin on her stomach.

Laughing gaily, her face to the side so that her profile was on the window, she didn't see me though I was only a table width away. She dropped to the sidewalk, skating backwards and off the curb in a kind of jump. I watched amazed as cars swerved to avoid her and she flew as if by some second-nature trick right against the thrust of the traffic.

The black-haired boy pushing the chair had some difficulty

getting off the curb. Tipping to one side, the chair fell but the second boy bounced to his feet, taking off after the girl across the boulevard.

By the time I left the restaurant, the sky was glowing with the reflection of light like a sheet of dark canvas strung with tent-show bulbs. The image of the girl squeezing her body to the window like a laughing crucifixion kept coming back to me, her bare stomach trembling with her breath and the shiny metal ring in her navel chattering or scratching against the glass.

Walking slowly up rue des Belles Feuilles past Leefeldt's offices, I was startled suddenly when a large-headed dwarf seemed to lurch from the shadows. He stopped and raised the bared stumps of his arms up towards me. It took me a moment to realize he didn't have any hands.

I stepped back but he said, "Hello!" cheerfully. "It is good to see you!"

I stared at the skin overlapping the blunted bone-ends of his wrists, as if stitched there to cover the amputated end of his arms. The wide thick face resembled a child's cartoon chalked on a ball, and as I nodded vaguely, he looked puzzled. "I am Phil*lipe*," he said. "You are with the actor Claude Duval and the others who come to Cafe Leper—"

"Of course!" I said. "I'm sorry, Phillipe. You're one of the people we've been tossing."

He laughed. "Please do not say it too loud! The police now say that tossing is so illegal." I laughed a little with him. He said, "Except for the cafe we are out of work with no food for our children. The Interior Minister has no doubt food on his table for *his* children but he wants to stop us from earning a living! So you see how it is!"

"You were wearing gloves in the cafe," I said, reaching into my pocket. "I'm sorry I didn't recognize you. I didn't realize you are without hands."

"The gloves are too much trouble to wear when I am not in the tossing," he said. "In the circus I wore baseball mitts that I painted like skin and it was very funny. The children all laughed.

Now I wear padded gloves only for protection when I hit the mattress. I have to strap them to my shoulders and it is very awkward, you see—" He thrust one stump towards me, turning it slightly to show the backside. I could see a small concave area like a little soup ladle or hollowed-out pocket. By contracting muscles in his arm he made the pocket move, open and sort of close like the mouth of a grotesque fish. "The *law* dictates," he said, "but does not say where someone as I can make enough to eat! The dirty bastards fail to face the fact that a shrunken man such as I am noneth*less* a man who must *also* eat, as must *my* children the same as the bureaucratic motherfuckers!"

"I couldn't agree more," I said, placing a handful of francs in that shallow spot in the dwarf's stump. Drawing back his arm, the other stump brushed the money into his coat pocket. Thanking me with exuberance, he said, "I hope to see you at Cafe Leper soon, monsieur!"

The damp air clung to chipped, painted walls and soft plaster as I stepped into a bistro near the hotel de Longchamp. Standing inside the door as if huddled against the chill, a tall transvestite in red plastic stared down at my cowboy boots.

"Ahhh!" he said, pursing his lips thick with gloss and showing uneven teeth. "L.A. or Texas?"

"L.A." I said. The colored lotion he'd spread down his neck was streaked with sweat, and beneath the pale coating, the pinched-up, pocked skin of his chest showed scars as if he'd been stabbed with a small knife.

"Three-hundred francs?" he whispered. I stared at the sweat leaking from his scalp beneath the wig. His skin had a green cast in the neon while dots of silver he'd stuck around his eyes by some sort of paste, glittered on the nodding face. "I will show you a good time for three-hundred francs," he said.

I shook my head. "No thanks," I said.

"Two-hundred francs?" he asked.

"No." I just smiled a little.

"Okay, John Wayne—" he said, raising one red-gloved hand and pointing the first finger like a gun. He flicked his thumb for the hammer and I looked at the chrome ring on the middle finger. It had a moon face on it. "I have to shoot you," he said. "Hey, I'm a good lay–I got tits and ass and I need to get some money. Whatta you say to me, mister L.A.?"

Again I went into my pocket, peeled off some francs and stuck them into his gloved hand, aware of the hole in the palm. He hadn't expected as much and the penciled brows arched up. He said, "Take me with you, mister L.A., and I'll give you a good blowjob."

"Forget it," I said. The transvestite walked out, looking around once to sing something back but I just waved a little and ordered a glass of wine. It had a bitter taste like metal.

Around the corner on rue de Longchamp, I went through the hotel doors wondering if the girl would be skating on the marble. David, the Japanese clerk, was on the phone and I tipped my hand to my lips. He smiled, shaking his head. "No saki tonight," he said, pointing to his watch. "I am going to watch your interview on television upstairs."

The elevator clanked to the second floor sort of tipping back and forth, and when I slid the door open I saw the two young prostitutes I'd seen earlier on the Champs. I smiled and said, "Are you ladies following me?" They giggled and I gazed at the dark one's high black mane and her wide mouth. She showed her teeth–the top row shining with small silver knobs set through the bone.

"Perhaps you are following us?" she said. The pink-haired one had freckled farmgirl cheeks but eyes as dull as magazine cut-outs stuck to her face.

They followed me into my room and Blackie said, "Oh, this is a *little* room! There is only one bed."

"There's only one of me," I replied.

"You are a lone *wolf*!" she said, shaking her mane which leaned to one side. She poked it straight in the mirror while I turned on the television, then opened a bottle of saki. Freckles sniffed and swallowed as Blackie's top and skirt dropped off. She jiggled her breasts in a black brassiere and pinched Freckles, horsing around on the bed.

I sat on the edge and felt Freckle's skin because it didn't look real. It was more like a rubber movie suit, and beneath the pink panty hose I noticed bruises across her thighs. She looked at me looking at the marks, and I said, "It looks like you've been whipped." She didn't say anything—only smiled slightly, her magazine eyes as dull as marbles.

I watched them tickle each other as they mumbled about money—more than I felt like giving, and though I handed them a thousand or so francs, when I showed more interest in drinking and the television, Blackie yanked on her clothes for an exit. They jabbered about meeting somewhere in Pigalle while I evened the tracking on the tube for *Paris Confidential.*

Blackie took off but Freckles was wearing the same smile as when I'd asked if she'd been whipped. Sprawling on the bed with the pillows bunched behind her, she said she had a sister a block south and we could screw the sister, or I could see the two of them make it together. For another thousand francs we could both whip the sister.

"Forget it," I said, laying on the bed alongside the farmgirl. The show came on but she didn't seem to notice there were two of me in the room—one on the bed and the other on the tube. I found that curious, though on screen I looked stiff and unpleasant, my face etched with shadow and somehow pitted as if by grains of sand. The eyes bagged from lack of sleep, appeared to go blank at moments and the mouth kept turning up in a kind of involuntary sneer.

I glanced at Freckles and wondered what it would be like to put the gun in her mouth, cover her face with the pillow and pull the trigger. She'd pulled off the pantyhose and I was feeling her thighs, tracing the blue bruises with my finger tips. I couldn't get hard even with her mouth sliding around half-heartedly to show some satisfaction for the money. She had some residue of obligation, though, wasn't totally wooden despite the magazine eyes. I turned her around and squeezed the cheeks of the ass, the only part of her that seemed really interesting—really quite lovely.

Looking at her ass, I stuck my first finger into it and thought of Divi.

With my limp cock in her hand and faking a full-lipped pout, Freckles said, "You are not having fun?"

I said, "No. This is very boring."

"I will do whatever you want," she said. "What do you want me to do?" I touched her stupid-looking face. My step-daughter would look just like her a quick few years into the future. I pushed my fingers into her mouth, feeling her teeth and the insides of her cheeks. I felt under her tongue, and then deeper towards her throat. Gagging, she grabbed my wrist to keep me from going further. She held my hand and drew her head back. I put my face closer to hers. There seemed to be sparks in her eyes— the lids nervous. "Do you want to whip me?" she asked.

"I only have an alligator belt," I said. "It's too expensive—"

"I do not need an alligator," she said. "I have the whip—" She leaned forward over the bed and reached. The cheeks of her ass were flecking as she came up with a short, thick, crop-like rolled tube of leather. "You see?" she said. "This is the whip. And the handle of it is hard... Will you give me more money so you can whip me?"

She pulled up the top, showing me her farmgirl breasts. "But you cannot whip these tits," she said. "You can whip my legs and my ass. Will you give me five-hundred francs more?"

I reached to the chair where I'd draped my pants, dug in the pocket and brought out a handful of francs. I set it on the bed. "Take what you want," I said. She pinched out five-hundred, bunched the rest into her hand and reached it toward me. I dropped the money off the bed to the floor as she rolled over, spreading herself face down, her bare ass and legs flickering blue in the television light.

I stroked the handle of the crude whip up and down her ass, then cocked it back and gave a swing downwards. It knocked against on her ass and her skin jumped slightly. I hit her again, then again, and she didn't jump so much but seemed to tense herself, clenching the cheeks of her ass and stiffening her thighs with each stroke. Several swings across her backs of her upper thighs had the skin red and crawling with goose-bumps. She kept her face pushed silently into the pillows until she reached around for my hard cock. Turning over, she rolled to her side facing me, sort of folding in the middle, her head against my stomach to take me into her mouth.

Moment later I sank back into the pillows when she got off the bed. The cloth was wet from her saliva. She said it was time to leave the hotel—to find her friend in Pigalle. "We will not get in trouble in Pigalle," she said, "but I will get in trouble if I stay in this hotel." Did I want to come with them? she asked. I said no. She said, "You would watch the television and not come with me?" I said yes. She stood there for a moment, shrugged exaggeratedly then quickly left the room. I heard her clanking the elevator door.

Something apprehensive was making a mess of the air in the room, clouding it like a gas. I finished the saki and went upstairs to the third floor, to the Longchamp end of the building and rang the bell at Robert Kamp's suite. Rustling sounds, a bed creaking—someone saying something. The voice wasn't the girl's or Robert's.

Without his glasses, Robert cracked the door a little and pressed his made-up face inches from mine. The gold-colored eye-shadow was smeared onto his cheekbones and the lipstick was on his teeth. Gathering his robe closed across the front of his thin chest, he said, "Oh! Jake! What a surprise!" Beyond him into the cluttered room I could see David half-covered on the bed. "I certainly hadn't expected you," he said. "I am sorry—but I'm indisposed at the moment—"

"I understand," I said. "I was actually looking for the girl on the skates"

"Juju!" he said.

"The blonde girl in the picture—I ran into her in the lobby earlier today—"

Robert said, "She stayed with me last week... She had a sleeping bag. She won't be back now because they are videotaping something on the Metro or somewhere."

"Is she on call for tomorrow?" I asked.

"No, she isn't—" he said. "With Mark Lajos' delaying things—I don't know when we'll be on schedule. Maybe she will be come by tomorrow. She has a pair of shoes." He shook his head. "I never know about Juju."

I nodded. "Sorry to have bothered you, Robert."

"I loved the interview," he said, "and took notes for Mr. Leefeldt. We'll talk tomorrow, Jake!" He eased shut the door.

There was a tall black man behind the desk downstairs, poking at the phone lights with very long fingers. Something was wrong and he seemed confused. I didn't say anything.

Outside the hotel on rue Longchamp, I stood beneath the lights of the marquee, smelling the air for rain. I thought about the girl crucified against the window, and somehow writing it into the Japanese script.

Her skull was perfect and the line beneath her hair was as circular as the earth's curve seen from the middle of an ocean. I gazed past a glaring yellow video sign to the struts of the Eiffel tower stretched darkly against the sky.

The street was quiet.

Tossing dwarfs had been the only exercise I'd been getting for weeks, and for a couple of days my arm ached from whipping the pink-haired prostitute. But by the end of the week I was tossing the dwarfs with ease, the strain gone.

Eston Sthole, the still-photographer on *Sucant le Sang*, was another seemingly half-crazy American who'd lived decades in Paris under the shadow of an even crazier mother who owned the building they occupied. Like a sort of cut-rate Andy Warhol, Eston threw parties nightly, had introduced me to dwarf-tossing as soon as I'd hit Paris and bragged that he was stronger than me, so I'd wind up buying the drinks.

The cellar dive called Cafe Leper opened for general business after seven. Between five and six the big African gal, Sonia, who ran the places, managed to squeeze in some blackmarket dwarfs for a hundred francs a crack, cheap even for our private parties.

Situated under a long-gone Chinese laundry on a dingy street of shabby hotels and one-time opium dens, the joint had once been a hot spot for radio writers and war correspondents who'd crowded the crooked steps down into the ginmill hole. Even the post-war jazz posters had long since peeled off the stone walls.

Over years, the clientele shambled from an Apache club to an American biker beer bar, then a hangout for washing machine mechanics and taxi drivers on a gender switch. The dwarfs came in months before the law clamped down on the tossing.

Eston was hard to beat. He sent his fat dwarf sailing like a tin-capped bullet, right to the blown-up mattress on a raised platform. Pierre without any hands wasn't there, but my helmeted human football bounced and popped up with Eston yelling "Bravo!" Scrambling off the mattress running crookedly on stubby legs like wagging sausages taped to an egg, my dwarf's eyes stuck out and he laughed wildly as I sent him sailing through the air.

Exhausted, I couldn't lift him again. I clapped but my head ached and my legs felt shaky. Only four of us tossed but the clock raced and it was quickly time for Sonia to open the cafe. A film editor friend of Eston's threw a black dwarf named Shoeshine who missed the mattress and yelled about a dislocated shoulder.

"He fakes injuries," Sonia told Eston. "He's a dirty little moocher who's begging for sympathy and wine and more francs."

Right after seven one of Sonia's greaseball bouncers climbed the steps to unlock the door. The rest of us lined the dwarf's pockets and stomachs with francs and wine.

Since Eston'd won the toss again, the drinks were on me. We laughed and gulped but I hadn't been able to shake that cloud that'd crowded over me. I'd dropped a dozen pills since noon the day before, just after the rollerblade girl tagging after Robert, showed up in my office.

Robert had knocked lightly on the frosted glass door, then

came in with a fresh-scrubbed smile. I indicated the pages on the desk, saying, "Rewrites for tomorrow."

Lifting them almost reverently, he said, "I don't know how you write scenes on such impossibly short notice."

"It's the reason I'm in Paris," I said.

"And the reason you'll be in Tokyo—" he said, about to say more when the girl was suddenly alongside him in the doorway. She draped one arm on his shoulder and he said, "Please do not disappear. Mr. Leefeldt wants me, and then I'll take you to the set." He slipped an arm around her waist which she eased out of with a roll forward on her skates. The red shorts hugged her hips like another layer of skin. "Stay here—" Robert said. She nodded and he turned quickly.

"So we meet again," I said to the girl.

"Yes," she said, edging back and forth on the skate blades. "We meet again."

"Those certainly are beautiful skates," I said.

"They are Nitroblades," she said.

"I gather that's a good brand—"

"It is a *very* good brand," she said. "They were a very expensive present to me." I smiled, nodding. She said, "You are the second writer I have met that is famous."

"I'm flattered," I said, "but I'm afraid 'famous' is not the right word. Who was the first?"

"Pablo Passola," she said and pursed her lips as if expecting a kiss.

"Passola the poet?" I asked. "He must be quite old by now."

"Yes," she said. "Pablo sent me a book inscribed to me because he wrote a poem about me two years ago in Marseille."

"Passola wrote a poem about you?"

"I know it by heart," she said, and recited the poem rapidly in French, then in English. "It means I was a sudden sunlight that came like lightning into a dark place. Pablo said that it is a force like lightning, you see, and he said, 'sudden'—*tout à coup*! In the dark as though it is midnight, suddenly a *loud* burst of this force Pablo said was like the wild bird jumping up into the air—" She stopped talking when Robert appeared behind her. "I was reciting Pablo's poem for Monsieur Morgan," she said.

"Will you be at Cafe Leper later?" Robert asked me.

"Cafe Leper!" she said. "Why do you go to that place? There are no bands there anymore."

"But the dwarfs are good," Robert said.

She made a face. "Why do you throw the little dwarfs? It is against the law now—"

"Nevertheless!" Robert said impatiently. Come *on*, Juju—" " He whisked her backwards by the slim hips, and pushed her out of the office.

Turning from Robert and still looking at me, she said, "It was a pleasure talking to you again, Mister Morgan. Something in her eye—a kind of fixed glance held me. For a moment, sunlight through the window overlooking rue Belles Feuilles struck her eyes and they seemed to glow brightly for an instant. They left the office and I swallowed a couple pills Eston had given me the day before.

After the dwarf tossing in the cafe, I bought the drinks for Eston and the others. "I'll be at the flat later," he said. "Everyone's coming over—Mark and Marjorie and Claude. Are you coming? I want to talk to you—you're the only person I know who isn't crazy. The others and these foreigners—there's something wrong with them, Jake, some defect in the personalities. Will you be at the hotel?" He was making a quick stop with his spy camera to get some shots of a dog-fight, and I stayed at the end of the bar on the last stool, watching the steps where the only rays of daylight snuck into the cellar.

The cafe crowded quickly and I was on another drink when the girl came down the steps. She was in some kind of Dutch shoes that gritted on the stone steps.

I could see the ends of her skates sticking out of a black backpack she toted by hand. The orange tank-top tee-shirt was cut so high above her stomach it barely covered the lower halves of her breasts. Under the thin cotton, her nipples were thrusting like the ends of fingers with little lumps of metal pushing at the fabric. Below the hem of her short skit, her bare knees were like a child's, and she had an old fur piece slung over one shoulder and sort of swinging against her left.

The wood-soled shoes shuffled to let some people move around her, and gazing about intently, she spotted me and gave a head-rocking smile as though finding a lost-long brother.

The same gold eye makeup as Robert'd used seemed smeared around her eyes, with black penciling traced around them. Her whole body seemed to play as she came angling through the room, fingers and forearms touching against herself. Approaching me, her rhythm went lazy—swaying as if somebody'd said 'Show me a slow dance.'

"Monsieur Morgan!" she said. I said hello and she stood in front of me, hooking her thumbs into the waist of the skirt. Each move or sway, her hands seemed to pivot, fingers brushing against that upper part of her crotch or the skin of her belly with the silver ring through her navel. "How exciting to see you so soon again," she said.

"How are things on the Champs?" I asked.

"With Tanyous?" she asked.

I wasn't sure who she meant. "At the hotel you mentioned film students—" I said.

"Ah, yes! That is Tanyous," she said. "Up and down the Champs and Al was on the ground with his camera—flat on the sidewalk. I came very fast and *jumped* over him!"

"It sounds as if the video will be a success," I said.

"That I will not know," she said. "But they are supposed to give me a copy tomorrow or maybe it will be next week. But I do not have anything to watch it on so I must go to Robert's again to see myself."

"There's a VCR at the office," I said.

"I would be afraid to take such liberties, Monsieur Morgan—"

"Please call me Jake," I said.

"Jake—" she said, hitting hard on the *k*. "It is like the *Two Jakes* in the Jack Nicholson movie?"

"That's right," I said.

"Have people always called you 'Jake'?"

"Yes," I said. "Most of my life."

"But your name was Jason in credits for the submarine movie," she said. "Was that the name your mother gave you?"

"Actually, no," I said. "It was my father. That's really my name but I've been called Jake for years."

"And I am Juju," she said. "I was called Ju-*gee* when I was little, which was a nickname. Or you say Juju like people say *ju-ju*-bee, for the gummy candy that sticks in your teeth."

I nodded. "A juju is also an object of magic," I said. "Do you know about magic? It's an object with magical powers venerated superstitiously—"

She stared laughing and I stared at her small teeth again, white and hard as porcelain. "Oh, I do not know about *magic*," she said. "All I know is people say I should be an actress in movies, but I don't know if that's what I should do. Sometimes think I would like to dance, and maybe be a dancer in the Crazy Horse Saloon, but I am too busy skating."

"Where are your friends tonight?" I asked. "The film students—"

"They do not come here to Cafe Leper," she said. "We go to the Red Egg where the bands play almost every night." She smiled. "But I came here to see you, Jake."

"To see me?"

"Oh, yes. Maybe I will throw the dwarfs."

"You're too small," I said. "They're as heavy as you are and feel like they're getting fatter."

"I am strong, though!" she said. "I can *sock* somebody but maybe it is hard to lift the dwarf—" She flexed her muscle for me and said, "Won't you buy me a glass of wine, Jake? I don't have any money!"

"I'm sorry. Of course," I said and waved to Sonia.

"My friends go to the film institute and are very impressed that I talked to you," she said. "I wanted to go to the school like Tanyous does, but I did not have the school records from my background. You have to have the documents to prove that you have gone to other schools." I nodded. "That would have let me go to school but I do not have the records. So here I am!"

"Well, I'm delighted you're here," I said, "with or without the records."

"When did you make the submarine movie?" she asked.

"A long time ago," I said, handing her a drink.

"I would like to see you act in other movies, Jake. You were very good. How many did you make before you became a writer?"

"Perhaps a dozen," I said. "I liked it but I felt I had other things to do—another calling, you might say."

"Like the call of the *wild*!" she said. "That is what I am. The wild girl!" She laughed. "Now you are writing *Sucant le Sang* about a wild *vam*pire!" She made a face, showing her teeth.

"Not much is left of the original script," I said, "that Mark Lajos and I planned to shoot in L.A.".

"Now that is where I want to go," she said. "It would be a dream to wake up in L.A"

"I'm not sure what sort of dream it is anymore," I said.

"But I have never been out of Paris," she said, "except to go to Marseille where Pablo Passola wrote a poem about me."

"How did you meet him anyway?" I asked.

"Through Robert who knows everybody," she said. "And I met Robert on the train going to Marseille! I determined to go to Marseille on my own and see the film festival. In Paris I spent all my time seeing movies, so I thought, oh, well, I should go to the film festival in Marseille and meet people who are *in* the movies!"

"So did you meet anyone except Passola?" I asked.

"I saw Peter Fonda and I met Patrick *Swazey* and they had so much money to spend," she said, "I said to myself it would good for *me* to be in the movies, too! But you see, I did not know how to do anything except skate. I am very good at skating—even on roller skates, and then I put on the rollerblades! Robert says I should be in the Olympics." She gulped her wine. "Pablo knew *every*body who was famous, and we walked on the beach. Because he was so old he had sore legs and would put his hand on my shoulder so he could walk better in the sand. He had a very big hand," she said, shrugged, her breasts wiggling. Standing so close to me, I could smell her and I liked whatever it was she had on.

"But I am wearing nothing!" she said. "Do I smell unusual?"

"It's really quite interesting," I said.

"Aha, maybe it is the tiger bottle," she said. "I have a bottle of perfume in my backpack—" She looked down at her feet disappointedly. "These shoes do not fit, you see. Robert gave them to me because they are from Amsterdam but I am so miserable I will take them off—" She pulled her feet out of the shoes and stood barefoot, shorter by an inch or two. Her toe nails were painted black. "Anyway," she said, "if I do not skate, I do not usually wear shoes."

I was staring at her stomach. "Did it hurt," I asked, "when the hole was pushed through your skin for that ring in your belly button?"

"Oh, it did a little maybe," she said. "They have to clamp the flesh and the needle goes straight through, making the hole so it is not crooked. If you do not have the clamp then it doesn't make a straight hole and pulls, and then it will hurt. This did not hurt as much as when they pierced right through my nipples—" She put her hands on her breasts.

"I could tell you had something there," I said.

"I have it somewhere else, *too*," she said mischievously. "But I cannot show you that ring!"

"Very interesting, I said. "Are you wearing it right now?"

She then took the rings in her nipples between her fingers, lifting them slightly against the cloth. "You see," she said, "a chain fits through these rings and then goes through the ring in my belly button. And then it gets put in the ring that is lower down—"

I was looking at her and she said, "Give me your hand. If no one is looking I can let you feel the ring—" She put my fingers against the small piece of metal in her crotch. She laughed. "I'm sorry. I have embarrassed you."

"No," I said. "It's most interesting."

"That ring is not comfortable when I skate, you know. Eston Sthole took pictures of the chain going through the rings and hooking to a collar that I wear around my neck. It is spiked like a collar for a big dog. But now I have lost the collar and I don't know where it is..." She pouted a little and emptied her wine glass. "This is good," she said, smacking her lips. "Eston took pictures of me wearing my skates but I was not skating, only posing with them on and wearing my silver chain and collar. He has not paid me for the pictures so I don't have any money—"

I flagged Sonia for another round. "Eston does not know anything about skating," she said. "He took pictures of me for the magazine but I have yet to *see* the pictures or even the magazine. I ask him and he says he doesn't know when the magazine will be for sale but he will pay me when it is published. Did he show you the pictures he took of me?"

"No," I said. "I haven't seen any pictures of you."

"He did not even give me copies of the ones when I am in my cowboy chaps and my hair like this—" She tugged her hair down in front, dropping her face so I couldn't see her eyes. "He said he would pay me but he is too busy taking pictures of dead people," she said. "He wanted to show me pictures of dead bodies, but I said I was not interested because I have *seen* a dead body—" She took a gulp of wine. "I suppose he will take my picture again when I am dead—but he says he wants to take pictures of dead people that are famous. He showed me pictures of the dwarfs you tossed. Did you see the picture of the Russian dwarf who has a large organ? Eston put a little hat on it and took pictures of the dwarf's organ wearing a hat. It was very obscene, Jake, and dis*gust*ing!"

"I never saw anything like that," I said.

"He probably does not show those to people but I imagine he shows *my* pictures to everyone." She stretched her arms upwards and the end tank-top came up against the base of her breasts. "Do you know Tanyous," she asked, "who plays the guitar?"

"I saw two boys following you," I said. "One was in a

wheelchair with a camera—"

"That is Al," she said. "His name is Al-something. Oh, it is some confusing Algerian name but he is called Al. Both he and Tanyous are envious that I have come to see you." She stared at me for a moment and said, "I hope you do not think I am putting a burden upon you..."

"Of course not," I said. "What do you mean by that?"

"Perhaps you are waiting for someone and I am taking up your time?"

"You're not," I said. "Would you like another drink?"

She seemed to think it over. "Will you buy me some cabernet to drink, Jake?" she asked. "I am so thirsty from walking in these terrible shoes."

"Of course," I said.

"I like red wine," she said. "Mark Lajos told us about a Hungarian wine that is dark in color like blood, and said it is called the blood of the bull. I will look for a bottle of that one of these days when somebody pays me the money they owe me. In the meantime I will probably starve to death like one of the dogs on the street—"

I laughed. She looked at me and laughed. Sonia placed two more glasses of wine. "And is this Tanyous in the movie as well?"

"No," she said. "He would *like* to be but he is not. He asks me to talk to people and convince them what a fine actor he could be, but while he plays the guitar he hasn't any other talents... Well, not many, I should say. He is very gentle and a nice person."

I said, "I gather this fellow Tanyous is your boy friend?"

She shook her head, fluffing her hair and looking around again. Her slender, long neck seemed to turn fluidly as though with little effort she could revolve it all the way around.

"He works at the Red Egg washing glasses and sweeping the floor, and then he plays with the band later. You must hear him play *fados* from Portugal—but he is not Portuguese. Do you like fado music, Jake?" I said I did and she raised her glass. "Salut!" she said, smiling.

Something very beautiful about her in a wild way, thin sort of hungry beauty. Something undomesticated. She even smelled wild. "Al has said that he comes here sometimes but not to throw the dwarfs. He is the roommate of Tanyous and works for the newspaper. He says he wants to be a writer but he does not write stories for the news, just does the proof reading for what they put in the paper. He knows who you are and he says that he admires you—that you are a very great writer."

I laughed. "That's very generous of Al," I said.

"I cannot promise his real name," she said. She sipped the wine and said, "I can't drink anymore of this. I'm sorry. I think my stomach is too empty."

"Perhaps something to eat?" I asked.

"Oh, yes, I could eat something," she said. "But you are sure you not waiting for somebody who is to join you?"

"She's already arrived," I said.

"No!" she said. "Do you mean somebody is waiting for you now?"

"It's you," I said. "You said you came to see me." She stared at me and then giggled. I patted her warm and rather damp hand and said, "I was planning on having something to eat and going back to the hotel to work."

"The Ronde-Point de Longchamp," she said. "Robert will not move out because he is such a creature of habit. It is so far on the other side of the river, too, and I am happy on Saint Germain. That is where I *like* to be!"

"What about Cafe le Braqu on the Quai? Would you like to go there?"

"That is a very fancy place," she said.

"No, it's not *that* fancy," I said. "It's rather—well, comfortable—"

"Se-*date*," she said. "You are a very sedate gentleman, Jake."

"I don't know how sedate I am—" I said.

"Oh, you are," she said. "You wear gentlemen clothes and I see pictures in magazines and on television of people in Beverly Hills and New York that are dressed like you."

"Creatures of habit," I said.

"I do not mean that *you* are old," she said, "but you dress the way people used to dress a long time ago..." She took another swallow and said, "You know, Jake, if we cross the river and walk down rue Dauphine we can go to a place that has fish and clams. I think they have the wine that Mark Lajos says is red like the bull's blood." Again she made a slight, pouting look. "It is not expensive and I am glad because I do not have any money! The film students promise to give me money since I am the star of the video but they still have not given it to me."

She left the clog shoes on the bar floor where she'd stepped out of them, and climbed the steps barefoot. Outside the door, an Arab breast-feeding a brown infant caught Juju's arm and said something I couldn't make out. Juju asked me if I had any francs to give the woman. I pulled out some money and reached it down to the woman who looked blind.

Walking ahead of me, sort of weaving a snake-like trail, Juju said she wondered how the Chinese women wore such tiny shoes for so many years.

"Their feet were deliberately deformed from childhood," I said. "They were made that way." Juju kept turning her face and squinting into the sun to smile at me.

"I like to walk with you," she said.

I said, "I'm enjoying the walk with you."

"What do you do at nights in Paris?" she asked. "Do you go to parties where the famous people go?"

"Usually I work," I said. "I eat. I drink and wander around."

"Robert told me you are divorced from the actress Ann Michaels," she said. "I asked Robert if someone was with you in Paris."

"What else did Robert tell you?" I said.

"He told me people say you are having an affair with someone's wife only because you had an affair before she got married." I laughed. I said I wasn't having an affair. Skipping ahead of me, Juju said, "But if you go to Eston Sthole's parties often you are bound to meet somebody to fall in love with you."

"I haven't met anyone at Eston's who's likely to fall in love with me."

"What about the star of the picture—Marjorie Lee? She is beautiful and she is from London."

"Right now," I said, "Marjorie Lee is pretending to be the girl friend of Mark Lajos."

Juju spun around, almost dancing. "Robert said you came up to his room and asked about me," she said.

"That's true," I said. "I wanted you to bump into me again."

"And so I have bumped into you!" she said, laughing, glancing over her shoulder as though expecting someone behind us. She walked backwards a short distance, bent down to gather leaves, then threw them into the air, sort of running beneath them. Dashing ahead playfully, she'd then turn around and I had the distinct feeling she went backwards to see the street behind us.

"You *are* the girl friend of this Tanyous at the Red Egg?"

"Oh," she said, "you see, he is in love with me, I imagine. That's what he says to me, but I am not his girl friend. Right at this moment, at this time and in this day I am not anybody's girl friend."

"So you are free," I said. "As free as the flying bird."

She said, "And what about you, Mister Jake? Are you a free bird as I am?"

"You bet," I said.

"So that makes two of us who are free at this time," she said.

Across the bridge, we walked along Saint Germain to rue Mazarine, then another short block to rue Dauphine. Juju stopped at windows—panting comically, making fun of me or laughing and pointing. She stood as if hypnotized before a hardware window stacked with Levi jeans, but then I noticed her glancing at the reflection of the street on the glass.

A few doors further she darted into a little cafe. The walls were lumpy plaster painted dark green. She said, "Please hold my backpack and I will be right back!" then scampered between the small tables and in and out of the little cubby holes.

Back after moments, she stood with her hands extended

helplessly. Shrugging, she said, "I thought some friends were here so you could meet them, but they are not here and that makes me nervous."

Handing her the backpack I said, "You've bitten your fingernails."

"Because I am very nervous," she said. "Tanyous says I am the most nervous person he has met. Not that I am shaking with the jitters, you see, but that I have so much energy I have to keep flying wherever I go."

"How long have you known Tanyous?" I asked.

"Oh—two months—maybe less than that." She shrugged. "Maybe it is longer. I am not good at remembering time. I would hear him sing and we would talk a little because he knows Robert. I have known Robert longer who is not a boy friend because Robert does not like girls to sleep with." She stared up at me. "We can go along Saint Germain to eat something," she said. "Don't you think so? This does not look so good now."

"Is there someone in particular you're expecting?" I asked.

"No," she said. "I am hoping to find the film students to get the money from them."

"What about this Tanyous?" I asked.

"I am not looking for him," she said.

Outside on Dauphine, as we headed again to Saint Germain, she smiled weakly and sighed. "Sometimes I have sad memories, Jake. Do you ever have sad memories?"

"No," I said. "What sad memories do you have?"

"I am reminded that Eston Sthole has pictures of my friend, Jean Paul Vermond after he was dead. You know, only the police are supposed to have such pictures. And everybody knows that I was the model for some of Jean Paul's famous works."

"I'm not sure I recognize the name," I said.

"My friend was very respected," she said. "An artist people know in Paris. The big studio on rue de Seine is only a short ways from here. So many times I have been here going to Jean Paul's. But you see, they kicked me out when Jean Paul's mother— a very old lady—came to tell me I could not stay in Jean Paul's studio.

It is very sad to discover the body of someone who has loved you and trusted you. He killed himself."

"That's terrible," I said.

"He committed suicide," she said. "I still have not overcome the grief, and it disturbs me that Eston has pictures which did not belong to him. He said he supposedly got them from some person with the police, but I did not see the photographs and told him I hope I never do.

"I can imagine," I said. "I'm sorry."

"Jean Paul's mother who is a *bitch* hounds me and has the police follow me because Jean Paul loved *me* and his possessive mother is very jealous—"

We were on Saint Germain and she suddenly bounced up, calling to someone across the boulevard at cafe Deux Magot. "Will you wait for me, Jake? I must say hello to some friends—" Dropping the backpack, she sprung ahead, bouncing barefoot between the cars and motorcycles, the soles of her feet flashing black as she ran. I picked up her backpack and sat on a bench.

For several minutes she lingered around a sidewalk table crowded with young people, once or twice waving to me across Saint Germain.

It was like a performance art piece the way Juju danced back through traffic, darting in and out of moving cars. Breathless and excited by the time she reached the bench, her earlier sadness or disappointment had vanished. "Fernando has a new camera!" she said, and quickly opened the backpack. She maneuvered out the rollerblades as I jokingly asked if any of the boys at the table were supposedly in love with her. She laughed, shaking her head but showed a somewhat disagreeable face.

"Deux Magot is for very proper people," she said. "It is for people like you, Jake. But those are actors and a musician I know from the Red Egg. I said I was having 'cocktails' with Jake Morgan who writes the movies and they are very impressed."

"It's my pleasure," I said.

"When you say things like that," she said, "you are proper and should be sitting at Deux Magot—" She smiled, brushing the dirt off her feet and wiped between her toes. Before pulling on the same kind of black socks she'd worn at the hotel, she held one to her nose, smelling it.

She then slid her feet into the skates, fastened them and stood up. Gathering her backpack, she whirled around in a tight circle. I asked her where she was going, and she said, "Fernando is taking pictures. He has a telephoto lens and is taking pictures of us right now, Jake—"

I watched, amazed, as she suddenly sailed off the sidewalk into the traffic on Saint Germain, zigzagging the intersection and heading for the bridge.

Someone on the street yelled as she raced past. "JuJu! Over here, JuJu! Come back!" Someone from Deux Magot hurried after her—and another was starting up a motorcycle. In moments she seemed to have disappeared. She'd sprouted wings.

I waited for and several minutes, thirsty for the drink we'd travelled for, wondering if she'd be skating back.

No longer hungry, I got to my feet and walked carefully across the boulevard.

A horse's head painted gold hung over the door to a dingy meat market on the street floor of Eston's building off rue Serpante. The rusted iron gate at one side opened to gray steps climbing up into the structure.

The second floor, a dim hall the color of algae, was lit by ornate frosted fixtures Eston's aging mother kept supplied with low-wattage bulbs. A crooked, one-eyed woman, she often answered her door without the black patch and her gray-filmed, blind eye showed as dull as a stone.

Almost deaf, she heard few sounds beyond the walls of her flat which ran the length of the second floor.

I'd glimpsed her clapping in the hall at two small, hairless dogs—yapping and snapping, their bony hides as bare as pigs.

Once when she chase the dogs into her kitchen, I saw chunks of raw meat on a bread board and a long silvery fish shining in the glare of an old television somebody'd rigged incautiously to an overhead fixture.

A left turn at the rear of the second floor hall sent one up another wide flight to the third story—Eston's apartment. I could hear loud surfing music hammering against the wood panels of his door. The sporadic, near-hysterical laughter of Mark Lajos shot up above the others, and after I knocked hard a couple of times, Marjorie answered the door. "It's Jake!" she cried. "Jake's here!" She looked so stoned her skin had taken a tint of blue from her blood going bad. "I thought you'd given us up, old Jake!" Her arms flung around my shoulders, pressing her chest to mine. The blouse, unbuttoned, showed the weight of her bullet-shaped breasts in a brassiere the size of a sling-shot. Half the shots in the movie captured the minute details of her tits while her back—so acne-pocked—was never photographed from any angle.

After planting a wet kiss on my mouth she staggered back a few steps to dance in a circle and almost toppled. The black Fifties pedal pushers hugging her seemed covered with lint and cat hair. She puckered her mouth, singing "Love me, love me, love me—" as Mark's sweaty face peered up half-hazed in the musty Turkish cushions.

"Jake's back!" said Che Che, a transsexual perching in purple filigree beneath Eston's gilt-framed prize—a pre-War portrait of Adolf Hitler.

Eston came out of the kitchen grinning with cups and a vodka bottle. "I didn't think you'd be coming!"

"I didn't think I was either," I said. "Too much work—"

"That's bad, Jake."

"Claude's in the can," Marjorie said. "Puking his guts because Che Che's scored some absolutely fucking sen*sat*ional coke, Jake. You must share if there's any left—these fucking *hogs*—"

"Oh, Jake—oh, Jake," Che Che said, rolling inch-long lashes to my face and pleading behind a casual smile. "Jake the rake's here so say hail-mary's and our-fathers. Say 'Hello, Jake! I'm in love with you!'"

"Me too you," I said. "God made us for one another."

"Oh, no, not *him* again," Che Che said. "Let's get stoned and go kill god! Do you think he takes it in the ass, Jake? But I love him because he's showed me the way to the tits and ass I've got. Please sit by me, Jake, so I can worship at your feet?"

"Forget it," I said. "I don't need any more worshipping—"

"No, Jake sits here," hunchbacked poet Paul said. "He hasn't had a taste yet."

Mark was bunched with the pillows, one arm draped with a squat joint burning and a leg sticking over the arm of the sofa, the shoeless foot wagging nervously.

The hunchback's head was like some smaller man's that'd been fitted onto to a squat lumped torso; a slim, floor manager's face except for sneaky eyes.

"I want more," said Marjorie. "Paul—I want *more* if you're going to give Jake some. I just can't fucking get high on this shit!" She flopped down half on Mark, throwing her legs apart, one hooking to a hassock. In seconds she bounced up again and stared into my face, nose to nose. "I was being fa*cetious* about how *good* it is!" she said. "If you want to burn a hole in your bloody fucking nostril without getting *high*—"

"It's Che Che's dope," Paul said. "Ask her—"

"He's not a *her*," Marjorie laughed. "She hasn't got a *pussy* so don't call him a her!"

"Marjorie will show you what a cunt's all about," Mark popped in. "You got to see if you can match this one, Che Che!" His squinty eyes shot to me and his grin parted like tin sliced with a can-opener. "I can see where this is heading!" he said, blinking despite the low lights and candles. Eston was motioning me into the hall.

"Oh, oh!" Che Che cried. "They're going in the *bed*room!"

"Jake's a heterosexual!" Mark said, laughing. "He's true blue in the stew, aren't you Jakey boy? Maybe a little pedophilic around the phallus—"

"What's that mean?" I said.

"My god, Jake—*you're* the writer—" Marjorie said.

"It means you're all fucking *loaded*," Eston said.

"It means we all watched Paris Confidential!" chirped Che Che. "Mark doesn't like being called a *child* rapist—"

"Fuck off you queer! You fucking fruit!" Mark cried.

"All of you shut up," Eston said. "You'll have my fucking mother up here."

"Oh, honey," Che Che said. "Such a delirious prospect."

"Jake," Eston said, shaking his head. "I want to show you some stills—"

"More *stills*," Marjorie said. "I want to see the *foot*age!"

"You can't," Mark said. "Nobody sees the footage except me and Jakey boy—and of course our dear godfather and our Nipponese princess—"

Laying lines of coke on a small silver tray, the hunchback said, "We don't know about *Eston*, but come back, Jake, and get a little hit before you and Eston—"

"Hit the sack!" jibed Che Che.

"Oh, stop it," I said to the transsexual, and bent over Paul at the couch. Sweat from the lump on his back had soaked through the corduroy shirt. He smelled of chemicals and cologne, aftershave or the hair spray that had plastered the thin rat-colored wisps over his peeling scalp. He handed me the tray and a silver straw. I stuck the end in my nose and snorted. "Jesus," I said. "That stuff hits hard."

"Don't call on *Jesus*," Che Che sang. "Call on *Che* Che—"

The bathroom door opened and Claude stuck his face into the hall. He stared at me strangely for a moment, then said, "I got sick, Jake. It was the chicken we ate on the set—"

Che Che shrieked. "You ate that little morsel? Oh, you're so naughty, Monsieur Duval!"

"I did not eat any Jujo!" Claude barked. "So stop saying it!" I glanced at Eston.

"It's a two-syllable word, Claude—Ju—*ju* ," he said.

"As in Ju-ju-bee," I said.

"To hell with that!" Claude said. "Dirty fucking Leefeldt is the cheap asshole—rotten fucking food, Jake. Robert says he gets a deal—I don't think it's chicken, Jake—it's some dead fucking bird—" He shut the bathroom door.

"He shot up with Mark and he's sick," Eston said to me. I could feel the ends of Marjorie's tits at my shoulder blades.

She said, "Mark's got a serious hole in his nose, and we're going to get some surgery as soon he finishes the picture."

"As soon as we get to Tokyo!" Mark called out. "We're doing another picture for the Japs—" he said. "Right, Jakey boy?"

We were at table pushed against the wall in the cluttered path between Eston's kitchen and stuffed living room. Marjorie had stepped around me into the little alcove to grab a jar of pickles. The edge of the table pushed at her upper thighs and she was bent somehow, her rear end naked under those pants—no panties. For a moment I thought of moving her by the arms out through the kitchen door. We'd be gone in seconds. I put my hand on one cheek of her ass and squeezed and then ran my fingers down the crack, feeling her heat. She had the pickles and turned around saying, "Eat one!" She reached it into my mouth. Munching one herself, she flopped around loose-limbed, bouncing back to the living room like her joints were elastic.

"Come here, Jake," Eston said. "How are you, my friend?"

"Good," I said. "Better now."

Almost whispering, he motioned me to the end of the hall. "You're here through all the post-production, aren't you?" he said. I said I thought so. He said, "And how long before you'd go to Japan?" I said I couldn't say. He nodded, smiling, took my arm and led me a down the hall towards his darkroom. "I don't want the others to hear me," he said. "If you're staying in Paris you might want to see the little attic apartment upstairs. My plan's to use it as my own space and open this floor for the business, but I'm doing two more *movies*, Jake. I mean, not that it's such a long-range plan but there's nothing I can do until Spring. I understand you've been looking to get out of the hotel—I mean, if you're serious about finding something—"

"Sure," I said.

"You're aware of what these seventeenth century Left Bank garrets are going for?" he said. "Not what somebody might *pay* for one, but just the sheer availability—" I nodded as he took my arm, ushering me into his darkroom. He shut the door and I stared at the stacks of prints piled about. One on top was one a proof sheet of Juju and I picked it up. "I was with her this afternoon," I said. "She came in after you took off, and told me about the pictures for a magazine. Is this some of it?"

"Yeah, a couple of those are for the magazine," he said. "But she's going to be on the cover of my coffee table *book*, Jake. Don't let anyone know." He brought out several other black and white proof-sheets.

I said, "She says you haven't paid her."

"Shit," he said. "Our deal's when I sell the book, Jake. I've got a publisher hot, but we just haven't hit the sack. I've even got a damned American house ready to bid."

"What do you know about her personally?" I asked.

He shrugged. "She's Robert's friend—sort of girl to girl. He brought her to Leefeldt who's used her in the picture for the part you wrote in. Nobody had to convince *Mark*, of course, but right now his dick's tied to Marjorie. Oh, he's *ogling*, you understand, but with Marjorie on deck, well, after all, she's a fucking maniac like Mark. She's staked a claim on him and he's comfortable for the moment. I mean, he never knows who's looking over his shoulder to see what a sex fiend he is." He handed me another proof sheet. "You like it? Dig it: clear plastic panties and rollerblades! Aren't they *mar*velous, Jake? Her little pussy was shaved here and she's got a *ring* it—" He handed me a magnifying glass. "Her cunt's like a child's, but she comes like this incredible *vamp*—this sex image or something just reeking to get laid! Claude said she fucked a *dwarf*, man!"

"He's full of shit," I said. Someone was knocking on the door and we heard Paul yelling at Che Che to let them in. "We are *busy*!" Eston called back, sliding the bolt. I stared at the pictures. "She's got the most beautiful little tits in Paris," he said.

"An interesting quality," I said.

"*In*teresting?" he said. "You can call it interesting. It's a *quality* right off the wall. Scary's more like it. You get a feeling from a subject—I mean this pint-sized Ma*donna* quality—the whore or maybe this lack of *innocence.* See how she's on the stool? Crawling around it like a contortionist or a goddamn snake. She flowed right into what you're looking at—sort of ab*stract* maybe. I had a seamless black drop and she said it was boring. I told her I had spray paint and she could decorate it. She did, squatting down in those plastic underpants with her hat on her head. She actually was going to have an *or*gasm in these shots and I was going catch her face as she came. But—it was weird—I started getting turned *on* and I suppose it showed so she shut me off flat."

I nodded.

"A few of the one's you're looking at," he said, "the black and whites with her leg crossed over—you see she's shaved and there's just a hint of her cunt showing—these go in the book. That one in black leather chaps and see-through panties is the *cover*, man, for *Children of the Night.* I might add she's thrilled about it."

He handed me another proofsheet. "These are while she's painting whatever graffiti's that's supposed to be. I mean, look at it. She's got some wild sort of native bizarre artistic talent or maybe she just osmosed it from Vermond."

"She told me he killed himself," I said, "and she'd found the body."

"She was one of Vermond's models," Eston said. "I should say the last one. He'd had a few before her and they sort of developed into live-in situations—for as long as they lasted."

"She said she called the police when she found him dead," I said.

"Yeah, suicide," he said. "I've got a couple shots of his body from the morgue, Jake, before he was officially released, you understand, to the private mortuary." Eston came up with another folder. "*No* one's seen these, Jake. They're for a book I've got cooking with a British publisher—"

One shot showed a sheet-covered body on the morgue gurney,

the face and feet sticking out, and the photo was of the bared upper torso to the waist. "These are before the autopsy, Jake. You can see the marks on Vermond's neck from where he hanged himself."

"He doesn't look very young," I said. "I'd somehow thought he'd be younger."

"Fifty or somewhere around there," Eston said.

"Why'd he kill himself?" I asked.

"Damned if I know," he said. "He had several shows last year. A lot of publicity, Jake... A lot of fucking money behind the guy. Your friend Samson knew him."

"I haven't seen old Sam since I've been here," I said. "I feel guilty as hell about it."

"Well, you'd better see him soon, Jake, before I'll be taking *his* picture. He's dying, you know."

"I knew he was sick," I said.

"There's one *truly* famous man," Eston said. "The last living master of the old Grand Guignol."

I handed him the proof sheets which he slid into a folder and filed. He then unlocked the back door of the darkroom and I followed him into the third floor hall. We walked to the end and turned left and started upstairs under an ogee-shaped arch. The narrow hidden stairway lead up a curving flight. "Like in a castle," he said. "Dracula waiting at the top for us..."

Almost out of breath at head of the stairs, we stopped on a tiled landing somewhat wider than the steps. Eston fitted a key into a plank door, saying, "Isn't it wonderful?" He turned the key and the door handle.

Though only half a floor at the fourth level, the garret stretched the length of that end of the building. "The rugs are Persian—very old, of course," he said, "but aren't they wonderful? All this antique furniture stays, Jake. The brass bed—the chair, the credenza. That little tiled table's worth a couple grand. You believe it?"

No pictures hung on the old plaster walls. Painted flat black, they reached to the front of the building beneath the roof and beyond Eston's balcony below. The vaulted flat-black ceiling angled down at the far end where a narrow glass door opened to a short balcony. Four floors below was rue Serpante. Straight ahead of was a panorama view of half the Paris skyline. I gazed at the high rising new buildings, and thousands of tile roofs and chimneys and pipes and turrets. I didn't say anything.

"Isn't this so much bigger than your room on Longchamp?" Eston asked. "And the skylight works—"

I looked up at wide old skylight, the width of the room and extending to the edge of the roof. An antique iron wheel chest-high on the wall operated the opening and closing. About six feet in sectioned depth, the thick, dusty glass panels ran the width of the room. Eston gave the wheel a few turns. Rusted, it creaked and stuck, and began to wind. The steel cables like small elevator lines ran up to pulleys the size of dinner plates. A chain from the wall to the mechanism beyond the ceiling tightened and the skylight began to open. Eston said, "Paris comes right down into the room."

"Yes," I said.

"You've got a little bathroom behind the door to the left," he said. The door was lopsided, and the room was walled with old white tile. Someone had painted the grout between the tiles with black enamel. An old iron tub with claw feet was gray with age, as was an oval mirror above a sink. "There is only the little stove for heating—"

"I'm not interested in heat," I said.

"You'd freeze your ass in the winter—if one stayed that long. If you want to convert anything, be my guest. Of course, at your own expense. So what do you say, Jake? I mean, until you're ready to go to Japan, and who know? Maybe you'll be coming back to Paris. You won't be going back to the States right away, will you?"

"I don't know," I said.

"Well, we can arrange it on a temporary basis," he said. "Work out something agreeable—acceptable. You know you'll get the godfather to foot the bill as long as you're here for the picture."

He abruptly took my hand and his shake seemed to rattle my sinews. His close-to-the-center eyes gleamed with satisfaction. "We've been good friends, Jake. That's why I've thought of you for this flat, like you can get me set up with the Japs, man. Maybe we'll be working together in Tokyo." Grinning, he cranked the skylight closed. We left the room and Eston locked the door. On the steps, he said, "We can be a team, Jake."

Back in Eston's, a pale, sweating Claude cornered us in the hallway from the darkroom. "Come in the front room, you guys," he said, "because Marjorie is going to do something—" He handed me the half empty bottle of vodka he'd been swigging on.

"What's our 'British bombshell' going to do *now*?" Eston said so the others could hear.

"I can't speak of it," Claude said. "Mark has talked her into it—"

"We better go see what it is," I said, passing the bottle to Eston.

"She's going to shoot up," Paul said. "We're doing speedballs."

"Oh, oh," I said.

"Wait a minute," Eston said. "If you're going to fucking die in my living room—"

"Nobody going to die in your living room," Mark said, sliding his eyes confidentially to Eston and then quickly to me. "Let her go ahead... Let her get high. She's quite a nut, you know. You think I'd let her die in the middle of a fucking picture?"

"What the shit are you saying?" Marjorie said, her arm reddish blue from the tube at her biceps. Paul was holding the needle.

"He says you're a nut," Eston said.

"Ah, yes!" she said. "Go *on*, Paul—let me have it, love—"

"I *am*," he said, his hump casting a shadow on the yellow wallpaper. "Hold still for Jesus's sake." Holding her arm firmly, he pushed the needle into her. She stared at it, then sighed slowly and looked up at me.

"What will you do if I die, Jake?"

Eston said, "I'll fucking dump you in a plastic bag once I shoot a roll of your ass on the floor."

"Will you fuck me first?" she asked.

"Fuck you?" I asked.

"Fuck me!" she said. "Fuck my dead fucking body. I want to get fucked when I'm dead."

"What about alive?" Che Che said. "You're clit get in the way?"

"Fuck off, you banger," she said. Mark tightened the tube around his own arm as Paul fixed another load. "I got a cunt!" Marjorie said. "A *cunt*!" She grabbed herself between the legs. "The rest of you've got fucking bloody nothing!"

"Go, girl," Mark said. "Tell us about it, Marjorie, babe—"

"I got a hot cunt and I can't get enough dicks in it sometimes. I got to get a fist in me—"

"You want to get fisted, baby?" Mark said.

"Fuck yes—but not by you ass kissers. You're a bunch of bloody assholes and I can do it myself!"

"*Okay*, baby," Mark said, pulling at Marjorie's peddle pushers, working them down off her hips. He glanced at Eston and said, "She's going to do it, man—"

"She isn't wearing any *under*wear," Che Che said.

"All the better to get a dick in me," Marjorie said dizzily.

"Pull them down," Paul said to Mark.

"I've got them down," he said. "How'er you feeling, Marjorie girl?"

"Better than I've fucking felt in a hundred years—"

"Oh, my," Che Che said. "She's a brown head. She has mousy brown hair on her pussy and it's pretty. You're really pretty Marjorie Lee."

"Thank you, Che Che, my sweet—" she said, rubbing her hands into her crotch. "Jesus *Christ*, haven't any of you got some bloody lubri*cation*?"

Claude said, "I saw some in the bathroom. I'll get it—"

"Doesn't mean I use it in *my* ass!" Eston said.

"Everybody knows you're a bloody bisexual," Mark said to Eston. "So it doesn't matter what you do with your asshole."

"Asshole—asshole," Marjorie said. "My fucking *ass*hole's as hot as my cunt. Gimmie something quick. Where's the fucking lubrication?"

Claude was down on his knees. He squeezed the tube onto her hand and she pressed it between her legs. "Phooey—it's cold," she said.

"Make it hot," Mark said.

"Put it on her fingers," Paul said. "She wants it on her fingers."

Claude squeezed globs over Marjorie's fingers. Her eyes squeezed shut closed and her neck muscles tensed as she pushed the lubricant into her vagina. Mark's mouth hung open as he stared at her hands and while Paul slid the needle into Mark's arm.

"Oh, god," he said. "Oh, *god*!" as Marjorie turned, twisting her rump on the couch. She worked her hands one way and then the other—her fingers disappearing between her legs. She laughed nervously, then began groaning—moaning, her eyes opening and staring down into her lap as she wiggled and angled her right hand into herself to the knuckles. Mark grabbed her left leg and pulled it up and then Paul took her other leg, mimicking Mark, raising it up so that Marjorie was wide open as she twisted her fingers into herself. Groaning, she managed to force the upper part of her hand inside, going deeper—easier now. At the same time, she reached her other hand under one raised leg and thrust three fingers into her rear.

Only the music and the sucking and sliding sounds of Marjorie's greased hands filled the room. Panting and licking her lips, mouth open, one hand was all the way into her vagina to the wrist.

We watched mesmerized as her other hand half disappear into her ass. Claude was hypnotized, working at himself in his pants like a ten year old. Saliva leaked from Mark's mouth and the hunchback was tipping over, almost lying down with his baseball head screwed towards Marjorie's crotch. She began to gasp, then cry out and seemed to quiver and shake into a sort of hysterical fit, thrusting her hands in and out of herself—wrist deep—crying out. She was going into some spasm and March said, "Jesus! What's she doing? Is she okay? Is she fucking dying?"

He tried to pull her hands out of her body. "God! I can't get them out! She can't fucking die in the middle of a picture! She can't die now—" Che Che and Mark seized Marjorie's wrist and yanked her greased hand out with a loud slurping noise.

She wasn't dying.

"She's on heaven's side of wonder," Paul said, pulling her hand out of her ass. She began to pee and we stood there watching her.

"Get a goddamn towel or something," I told Eston. "Go get something!" Claude broke his trance, jumped up and ran to the little kitchen while Eston and I picked Marjorie up off the couch. We carried her into his bedroom and placed her down on the chaise. I said, "Get something to cover her."

I put my hand on her chest, feeling the rapid fluttering of her heart. "Here—" Eston said, "get these towels under her ass and stuff so she doesn't get that vaseline all over the furniture." Her skin was racing between cool and warm as sweat rolled out of her pores. "The fucking idiot's going to *die*, man!"

"She's not going to die," I said, tucked the towels under her body. I felt excited—shaking in my stomach. "Go wet a washcloth and I'll put it on her face. Let her crash for awhile—there's nothing you can do."

"Will you stay with her for a few minutes?" he said, running the water

"She'll be all right?" Claude asked, sticking his head into the room.

"Thank god she isn't on call tomorrow," Mark was saying from the other room. "A fucking catastrophe if she's on call. You better ring Robert and make sure. She's a fucking *nut*!" His narrow eyes met my stare from the doorway and a slight, funny grin slid across the same tin-can opening of his mouth.

In the bedroom, I told Eston, "I'm going to cool her down a little. Let her crash—leave them out there." Eston left the room. I crossed to the door and pushed the lock on the inside handle.

When I placed the soaked washcloth over Marjorie's face, her open mouth sucked the wet material slightly between her lips. I pulled off the throw and looked at her naked stomach and legs. I leaned over her and kissed her mouth through the wet cloth, then opened my pants. I could hear Eston saying I was giving her a cool compress. "Best to keep her quiet—" he was saying and then someone turned up the *Cowboy Junkies.*

Marjorie's cunt was still dilated and greasy and half kneeling on the chaise, I pulled her left leg to the side, sliding in and out of her quickly. She began twisting her head back and forth, and when she started moaning, I turned her over onto her stomach, bunched the towel over her mouth and pushed my cock into her ass.

Juju lay on the boat's deck practically naked in her tiny pink panties, the dark crimson towel pooling out from under her like a puddle of blood.

She'd come on the boat with her hair colored fire red, tipped with points of black and green and crew-cut around the sides almost above her ears. The top stood up straight with a V-shape at the base of her neck. I asked how she managed to stiffen it up in dagger points, and she said with regular glue that'd wash out with hot water. "I don't want the color to go away too quickly" she said. "I like it!"

"I do too," I said. The cloth robe covering her had Robert's initials on the pocket and she smelled of sun screen and sweat from skating all morning before her call. Up and down the Quai for a slick-haired Italian who crouched for low angles as she'd raced on the walks, hands waving in the black kid cut-offs. Her bare thighs had glistened and she'd proudly showed her Calvin Klein cotton underpants by unzipping and opening the front of her shorts. Claude Duval kept staring at her and I felt sorry for him.

Robert was repairing her makeup, saying, "I'm not your agent,

Juju, and I'm not your personal makeup man! Stop smearing what I'm doing!" She giggled, chewing bubble gum and poked at his stomach. When he went to refill a spray bottle, she said to me, "I know that I might be asking for a great deal, Jake, but would it be possible that you could give me some advice at some time?" I asked what sort of advice, and she said, "About the movie business." Gazing up at me, she blew a large bubble with the green gum. It popped and stuck across her nose and mouth. Laughing, she picked it off and pushed it back into her mouth.

"Stop it!" Robert said. "You are messing what I am doing. Why don't you spit that gum out of your mouth?"

Whatever ideas I had, Juju said, would be most appreciated, she'd be most interested in talking about. The robe was open partly and I was looking down at her breast. She wasn't wearing the rings since the scene was the 'sacrificing of a virgin.' I said we should meet later—"Not at the Cafe Leper," I said. I suggested the little place on rue Dauphin. I said, "It's close to where I'm staying now."

"Yes," she said. "The apartment on top of Eston Sthole's building near Rue de Seine! I love the skylight across the front, and at night you can look up from the street and see the light shining into to the sky." Excited, she said, "We can meet at the Red Egg! You have not heard Tanyous sing and he will be playing with the band tonight when he finishes being the garbage man."

"That would be interesting," I said, "but I was thinking maybe a place near the flat that's quiet and where we can talk—later today." Her eyes were roaming over my face, those green lines in the yellow irises sort of revolving. I said, "The cafe on rue Dauphin?"

"Will you tell me your ideas?" she said. I just stared at her. "I am not good at time, but when would you like me to meet you?" I looked at my watch and said about five, but didn't think she was listening. She said, "I believe Claude Duval is unhappy because he is having troubles."

"What sort of troubles is he having?" I asked.

"People are saying his wife is no longer in love with Claude," she said. " I do not think anybody loves Claude. Only Claude's fans are in love with him. Maybe his wife is in love with you and maybe I should be the one that is jealous."

I was taken aback. She looked at me and blew another bubble. When it popped she sucked it back into her mouth and laughed. Gum covered her teeth and gums and her tongue. "So this is the latest scuttlebutt on the movie set?" I said.

"I too would be unhappy like Claude Duval," she said playfully, "if his wife steals *you* away." She chuckled a little, brought her face up close and kissed me on the cheek. "I will be at the cafe on rue Dauphin, Jake."

On the boat set, the assistant Bertrand Randolf said, "You want to look at this, Jake? Mark hasn't set the shot and he hasn't been here for a day and a half. Are we going to second unit the rest of the picture? The godfather says to shoot around him. How the fuck do you shoot around the director?"

I checked the shot and said, "Why don't you open this one close on the girl? We can cut to Claude, get his closeups, and then back to the girl's body. Shoot your close stuff here and go to the tracking."

"I don't think we can do it in the day," he said.

"Then we'll do the tracking tomorrow."

"The godfather'll shit," he said.

"Not a question of whether he'll shit, but who shall be shat upon." I smiled.

The cheap makeup person fussing with Claude's fake fangs, fitting the sharp porcelain plates over the eyeteeth, said the star was bleeding from the gums. The adhesive wasn't holding. "Jake," Claude said, "I'm getting a fucking irritation in my mouth." Sweat was leaking through he makeup.

"Take them out after the shot," I said.

Quietly, he slurred, "Jake, the young girl is too pretty to be running after these Iranians."

"They're film students," I said. "They're making a video."

Claude laughed as best he could with the fangs. "No, they are more than film students to this one, Jake, and that other character—that *creep*—" He glanced around the Quai. "He was here yesterday when we were up the river at the bridge."

"Who was here?" I said.

"The *creep*, Jake. He didn't come close and you could not see him with those dark glasses and a big coat around him like a refugee."

"Who was he?" I asked.

"He was hanging around by the bridge and when we moved down here the girl chased him away. Someone said 'Hey! Who is this guy?' and she ran and grabbed a stone and threw it at the guy! After that he was gone."

I said, "Don't worry about it. I'm going to be advising her."

"Well," he said, "you should advise her to keep her tits covered when she's not in front of the camera. She fucking shows her tits to people. That wop with the camera's been shooting them half the morning."

"That's a commercial she's doing," I said.

"Some commercial," he said. "Must be for *Hustler* magazine!"

I waited at the cafe on rue Dauphin for an hour but Juju didn't show. After some wine, I left the cafe heading west on Saint Germain, intending to go back to the flat-black garret but found myself drifting with a swarm of people, a motion spreading along the boulevards. For moments I felt an old spark—a kind of energy sputtering and flashing. Just for seconds it was like a ray of light knifing into some dark corner, and for some reason Mount Fuji rose up in my mind—sunlight and ice crystals melting and slipping.

Heading north along Saint Michel to Boulevard Du Palais, I spotted Juju at the sidewalk stall of the book shop. Her stuffed black backpack was on the sidewalk between the sloppy, old-style cowboy boots—steep stirrup heels and pointed toes being up at the ends like Thief of Baghdad slippers. They looked too big for her. She was flipping pages with her no-finger gloved right hand, holding another book in her left, against her ribs. In black from the big beret on her head down to the black tights covering her legs; a jet black blouse of long-sleeve rayon hung over the waist of her black skirt.

I let my breath out, feeling relieved for some reason and oddly disappointed for some other—aware I'd been holding it in since spotting her. I gazed at her ass and the metal-studded belt cinching her narrow waist, the end dangling halfway down her thigh. Her small face was all scrunched intently into the book as I came close to her, smelling a different perfume and the scent of her skin—or maybe the aroma acted as a catalyst with her own heat, which I could feel radiating from her like electric waves. The book beneath her left arm was an inexpensive collection of Rimbaud and I said, "That edition's got everything including his letters in the back."

"Oh, Jake!" she said, turning her head. "Where were you?"

"I was there," I said.

"On rue Dauphine?" she said. "But I did not see you. I went to look for Tanyous and Al but they did not have my money, Jake. They want to give me a radio and CD player instead, and I am very sad."

"You must have been there before I arrived," I said.

She nodded and began swaying her head and singing to the music piped over the stall about egg foo yung and King Kong in Chinatown.

"Well—" I said. "We're here. You look wonderful. Where are you going now?"

"I am supposed to see a photographer for another television commercial. Robert said they want me to skate and unwrap two rolls of toilet paper so that they are like streamers behind me. One is pink and one is blue. Robert says I am supposed to call them but another reason I am sad is because I don't have any money to call. This book is so good and I can't afford to buy it. In fact, I am starving like a dog—"

"What about lunch," I asked. "You had something on the set?"

"No, I was working on the deck and then I went to Robert's to make phone calls. I have not eaten today—" She closed her eyes—

remembering. "Yes–I had coffee this morning before the makeup." Her eyes darted to the book spread open before her. "This book is on sale," she said. "Have you seen this one on photojournalism? It shows the Buddhist monk burning himself and I have never seen these pictures..." She turned some pages. "Here are people being shot in the war... And a German they have hanged." I stared at the picture of the hanged man picture. She'd picked away pieces of the black paint on her fingernails and she kept shifting her weight like pacing while standing still.

It occurred to she'd intended to steal the Rimbaud book and she must have read my mind. She said, "I can't afford to buy books. It is ridiculous. Maybe I will come back and buy the Rimbaud because the godfather owes me money. He is supposed to pay me."

"He's always late paying," I said. "Look, Juju, let me buy this book–they're two for the price of one, you see. I'll buy two you can have both."

"But I do not want the photograph book. You can have that book."

"All right," I said. I felt very close to her. I wanted to hold her. "Now that I've captured you, how about getting something to eat?"

"On rue Dauphine?" she asked.

"No," I said. "I'd like to take a taxi across the bridge." Taking the Rimbaud from her other hand, I said, "We can make your phone call from a restaurant I'd like to visit. Are you on call tomorrow?"

She shook her head. "Not for the movie. I will work on Thursday and then I am through," she said. "Then I do not know what I will do." Her shoulder shrug was more of a twitch. "Maybe I will go to Los Angeles. Robert says this toilet paper commercial can make me famous and I can go to Los Angeles. But he also says this photographer is a terrible man and I must be careful he does not take advantage of me. He says I must make sure I get paid for the commercial. Right now until everybody pays me I will be broke." She laughed. "I will starve to death!"

"I won't let that happen to you," I said. "Let's buy the books and have dinner. Would you like that?" She nodded, rolling her eyes and grinning.

The books were bagged in a plastic sack with pictures of bookstall locations. Then, donning yellow plastic sunglasses in the taxi, she said, "I have enjoyed working in the movie very much, Jake. I do not know if I want to be an actress all the time, but I would be happy to work in another movie very soon."

"This was your first real movie?" I asked.

"Yes," she said. "Robert has been influential in keeping appointments but he says I do not appreciate his efforts. But I *do* appreciate it. Our friendship is not doing well at this time now that he is involved with David, who does not like me. But you see, Jake, it is David who is influencing Robert." She sighed. "So you see, I do not know who I am to turn to... Perhaps you will write another movie for a girl like me to be in."

Getting out of the cab at brasserie Ostier, she seemed to be limping, stooped to pull at the top of one boot and said, "I do not like these boots. I need to buy shoes or to leave my skates on and not take them off."

Salted beef and wine sounded good. She said she didn't care what she ate. We took a far booth by the window beneath a row of old boxing photographs, and scanning the menu quickly while I ordered a bottle of Beaujolais, Juju sighed again and asked what she should order. I said, "Anything you like. Whatever you want. I highly recommend the beef—it's plat du jour, or you might want to try the duck."

"The duck?" she asked, staring at the menu. The waiter pointed it out. She hesitated, then nodding slightly, said, "I will try the duck."

"Let me order that for you," I said. "It comes with a blood sauce similar to a gravy. If you haven't tried it—"

"Oh, I had duck in Marseille," she said, closing the menu. "I shall have duck." She looked very pleased.

"A good choice," I said.

"The duck I ate in Marseille was when I had dinner with Pablo

Pasolla," she said. "We saw a duck very high in the sky when we were on the beach and he told me what kind of duck it was but I do not remember. I remember the noise of the wings as it flew over our heads."

The waiter brought the wine, opened and poured it as Juju said, "I do not usually eat so much in the day because I skate all the time. Sometimes I get sick to my stomach. I was at Robert's uncle's place and I puked on the rug."

"Sorry to hear that," I said. "I didn't know Robert had relatives in Paris."

"Oh, it is outside of Paris and we took the train. I believe it is his real uncle," she said. "He is old and has a big red nose. He is stingy and saves newspapers which are piled into a room. Like Robert, he talks about Amsterdam. Robert is very dumb when he talks, but he has a fine brain and has been a good friend until now. He let me stay at his hotel but I am pleased to be out of there now."

"You've found a place for yourself?" I asked.

She shrugged. "Oh, I am still looking, you know. How long have you known Eston Sthole?"

"Since the gangster movie three years ago. We're also mutual friends with Mark Lajos."

She nodded cautiously. "Monsieur Lajos is another funny man—I do not mean funny as in a joke."

"Yeah, I said. "He's under a lot of strain."

"I have heard about the strain and how it involves you," she said.

I smiled. "More scuttlebutt from the movie set?"

Scooting a little towards the window as if shrinking down, her eyes darting past me, she said, "Oh, I wish he was not coming in *here*."

"Who?" I asked.

"That man who follows me sometimes," she said. "He is fat with a mustache and brown hat. Why is he coming in here? I hope he does not come to see me."

He was rather round, not tall, with a mustache and hat. Standing casually at the bar for a moment, he got a beer and smiled in our direction. "He's already seen you," I said. "Who is he?" The man approached our table with his beer mug, a rain coat folded over his arm. I was staring at him and he nodded, saluting a little. He offered a broad smile, showing large, rather far-spaced teeth darkened by tobacco.

"Ahh!" he said. "It is Juju!"

"I am not Juju," she muttered. "I am the ghost." She offered a polite smile as the man took her hand. He placed his mug on our table and patted her hand with his other hand, pinching the raincoat at his side by his elbow. His face turned to me and I rose slightly but he beckoned me to sit.

"This is Monsieur Jake Morgan," Juju said. "He has written the movie I am working in. Monsieur Morgan is going to advise me about working in the movies."

"Yes?" the man said. "I am very pleased to see you are receiving professional coaching, Juju. You are still working in the movie?"

"I am on call," she said, "then I will be skating in a toilet paper commercial for television. I am meeting with the photographer."

"Very good!" the man said, reaching towards me. "I am George Marlet," he said. "It is a pleasure to meet you."

I shook his hand and Juju said, "Moisure Marlet has written poetry—"

"But I must confess very badly!" he said.

"He will recite it if you wish," she said with a mischievous smile. "He can recite one about a crow that is lost in a storm."

The man blushed. "I am afraid this young woman is too generous with praise, monsieur. Any real writing talents I may possess are no doubt restricted to the police blotter. But I am a most sincere admirer of the arts," he said. "As a boy I dreamed of becoming a famous musician—"

"Yes," Juju said, "and he says he plays the clarinet."

"Again, I confess my playing is equally on par with my poetry. But we have visions and we dream," he said, patted her shoulder gently and then she jumped as a beeper sounded. The man laughed. "You are jittery, Juju!" Reaching into his jacket, he said,

"I must go. I'm afraid the muse that calls to me is but an electronic voice. It was a pleasure to meet you, Mr. Morgan. You are returning to the States when the film is finished?"

"No, he is not," Juju said. "He will be going to Japan to make another movie!"

"I'll be in Pairs a little while longer and then I must travel to Japan," I said.

The man shook his head enviously. "Ah, to travel," he said. "As I must do now—around and around in circles..." He nodded and bid us good day.

As he reached the open door, Juju said, "*Damn* him. He is a de*tec*tive, you know. A policeman and a snoop! He didn't drink his drink," she said. It was sitting on the table. "You see he didn't come in to drink—he comes in to snoop on me!" She picked up the mug and drank from it.

"You say he follows you?" I said.

"He does not follow me all the time, but I think when he has a chance he checks up on me."

"You're not on some sort of probation are you?" I asked.

"Oh, *no*," she said. "He follows me because of what I told you about Jean Paul being dead. This little man says they have questions that he does not have the answers to. So he follows me and asks *me* the questions about Jean Paul." She picked at the duck with her thumb and first finger, prying meat between bones. The last three fingers arched upwards free of the flesh and blood sauce. She had hands like a child. Little girl hands. The fingers seemed long when extended but appeared small as she pinched the meat away from the bones.

"What sort of 'questions' do they ask?" I said.

She sighed, slumping a little. "You see, I found Jean Paul after he was dead and it was *I* who called the police to notify them." She gulped at the wine, then sipped more of the beer.

"Go on," I said.

"I was at Jean Paul's on Rue de Seine—his studio was a shoe factory long ago. He lived in the upstairs and I skated downstairs because it was like a ballroom. Jean Paul was important and had lots of money—" Her mouth looked small, lips shining with the blood sauce. Her teeth were pink with it. The wine did the same as if the enamel was more porous than hard. She drank and said, "The big floor downstairs is where I would skate, and I would take the little elevator like the one in Robert's hotel, to go up because there is no stairs. I was skating for a long time, you see..." She paused to separate more of the duck, wolfing it into her mouth and crunching bones between her teeth.

Lowering her head, she spit the broken bones into her napkin. "When I was tired I went to sleep," she said. "I don't know how long it was... Maybe not long and I went up in the elevator because Jean Paul wasn't there, or so I thought, you see. I made coffee in the machine and put chocolate in it for Jean Paul. Then I put on the CD he liked, a Zydeco blues—Jean Paul had so many CD's, you would be amazed. He liked jazz, the big bands jazz, the blues jazz like Eston has, like he played while photographing me. Now *he* should pay me the money he owes me, too."

"I'm sure you will be paid," I said. "Back to this policeman who follows you—does he think you're withholding some sort of information?"

She nodded, wiping at her mouth with the napkin crumbled into a ball over the bones. "It is like a show on television," she said, "with the little police Inspector running after somebody—like in a Peter Sellers movie! Please, may I have some more wine? I am very thirsty."

I flagged the waiter.

"So I was dancing to the Zydeco blues, and that is when I found what had happened to Jean Paul. He had killed himself." She stopped eating and stared through the window for several seconds. "He had killed himself," she said again.

"And you called the police," I said.

"I talk to this awful man so much it gives me a stomach ache," she said.

"I'm sorry," I said.

She ripped more duck and dunked it into the sauce like a sandwich. Bunching the bread, she stuffed chunks of it into her mouth, keeping one arm protectively around the plate. "It was very sad," she said. "Jean Paul used a rope around his neck and put it over a pipe at the ceiling. But, you see, he had fallen down and he was on the floor behind the Chinese screen. I did not see him from the room where I was dancing." She sighed, raised the glass and drank, swallowing after the duck. The wine was very good, she said. I wondered how she tasted it gulping so fast and muddied with sauce and bread and bones pulverized between her teeth.

"So I have a heavy heart for Jean Paul," she was saying, "but this Inspector Marlet tells me there are complications. He thinks I am the crow in the storm, the innocent one yet to be free on its own. He supposes when that happens he will know what happened to the money Jean Paul had in secret places—suddenly there was *no* money—*poof*! The secret places were gone. This detective thinks I have ideas and I say to him that I do *not*. Do you know, he asked me to be *hypnotized*? He could question me when I am in a trance or a spell! He said, 'Oh, so you do not want to be hypnotized? It is because you are afraid of what you are going to tell me!'"

"What does he think you'll tell him?" I asked.

"How can *I* know what such a man thinks?" I refilled her glass again. "At first he was very nice," she said. "He was going to see that the big bad wolf does not eat me because I could not stay at Jean Paul's. This awful man did not fool me for long, Jake, though *he* believes I am still being fooled!" She drank wine. "It is a subject I am sore with like you would get sore from a horse all the time... When I get my money from Eston and from the godfather, Robert said he will get me a lawyer to put a stop to the police bothering me." She sat back, staring again out the window, then she smiled and looked at me. It was a different mask pulled down over her features.

"You told Marlet that you are not going away after the movie. Will you be staying in Paris long, Jake, before you go to Japan?"

"Until I finish the script for Japan," I said.

"You will stay in the apartment on rue Serpante?" she asked.

"Walking in the night under the skylight?"

"Yes," I said. "I might even keep the flat while I'm in Japan."

She was glad there were no elevators in Eston's building. Jean Paul had told her many of the old buildings were being condemned after installing elevators. I said I thought that could be a real problem since they had to tunnel some of it out of rock.

Up the curving tunnel past Eston's where it was too early for the usual party, Juju clung to the back of my jacket as we climbed to the top floor. The ceiling above the short landing was vaulted and two narrow snips of old wire-embedded glass let the light leak in like two brush strokes on the stone.

Inside the flat, she stared at the skylight and made cooing sounds in her throat like a pigeon. "If it was open and I was a bird I could fly away! I would fly to L.A.," she said. "Maybe I would fly to Japan behind the big plane that will take you to Tokyo—" Running her fingers along the tarnished brass of the footboard, she asked, "Is this bed yours?"

"I think it's been here since the previous century," I said. She plopped into the old chair which shuddered and creaked, and she quickly pulled off her boots.

"Can I use your telephone?" she asked.

"Of course," I carried it to her and she quickly dialed a number. She listened for several moment.

"It is busy," she said. She called again. "It is still busy. I will call later." She handed the phone back to me and gazed about the room. "This is like Jean Paul's space above the big studio only this is not as big. I don't mean *too* small, but I mean it is small compared to Jean Paul's. I stared at her green socks and asked if her toe nails were painted black like her fingernails. "Yes," she said. "Do you want to see them?" She yanked off one sock and wiggled her toes. Then she pulled off the other sock, got up and walked slowly around the room, sort of gripping the floor and rugs with her feet. "This feels wonderful," she said. "I can feel people walking a hundred years ago!"

She threw herself back in the chair and laughed, spreading her arms as she'd pressed them against the cafe window. "I could live here forever, Jake!"

"I thought you'd fly to L.A.," I said, "or maybe Japan."

"One must have a reason to go so far," she said. "Today I don't think I have a reason—" Spying the row of liquor bottles on the credenza. "You have the Greek drink—ouzo! It tastes like liquorice candy." I asked if she'd like some and she nodded enthusiastically. "The sideboard is wonderful, too," she said, watching as I poured two short glasses. "Jean Paul had a long cabinet that looked something like that except he had secret compartments inside of it." She giggled. "He kept hiding his money in these little places thinking nobody in the world would be able to find the money."

"Why did he hide his money?" I asked. "What was wrong with the banks?"

"Oh, he had money in the banks, too, Jake. I do not think he believed there was something wrong with the bank. But he put the other money in his hiding places. He had some funny ideas, Jake—I don't mean funny like you make a joke."

"I understand," I said. "Jean Paul seems to have had everything. Did he have a ring in his navel?"

"A *what*?" she asked.

"You have rings in your body," I said. "One the first things I noticed about you was the one in your belly button. You weren't wearing it on the boat."

"I have it in my belly button now," she said, "but Jean Paul did not have any piercing. He was funny—he said his body was made in the image of god's, but it was all right for me to get the piercing and wear rings in my body. I am wearing the rings now because I was not skating this morning—" She got up and said, "What I have to do is reach down into my skirt and unfasten the crotch of this top. Do you mind?" I shook my head. She opened the waist of the skirt and reached down, moving one hand between her legs and the other from the rear. Having unfastened the top at the crotch, she pulled it up along her body, baring her waist past the ring in her naval, and upwards over her chest. The rings were through the ends of her breasts, not actually through the *end* of the nipple but into the surrounding areola. She tugged gently on one of the rings. "It was sore at first," she said, "but now it does not hurt. Here, give me your smallest finger..."

I reached my hand to her and she took my little finger and inserted it through the ring. "You see?" she said. I stood there with my finger in the ring, the back of my finger against her nipple which was contracting against my touch. "It did hurt, but I like the way it is, and the feeling that it gives me. It was an accomplishment for me to have this done, Jake. See," she smiled, "it allows me to trust you..."

We stood in silence for moments. "I want to put my lips to the ring," I said. "Do you mind?" She didn't say anything and I lowered my face, kissed the ring and her nipple and then brought my other hand up to her other breast beneath the top. I raised the material and ran my hand down to the ring in her belly button, then back to the ring through her nipple.

"I do not have the chain with me," she said. "It fits through the rings and can be fastened to the nipples and then through the ring in my navel and I have the ring in my sex—"

"Do you have a ring in right now?" I asked. She nodded and I pulled the opened waist of her skirt lower on her hips until it slipped to the floor around her legs. I reached my fingers into her bare sex, feeling the ring through it.

I stepped her back gently to the edge of the bed, then eased her down. She lay her head back into the pillows as I kissed her breasts and got between her legs, licking her stomach and kissing her belly. I ran my tongue around the ring through the lips of her cunt and licked at the split. "Can you take it out?" I asked.

In moments she'd nervously removed the ring and I opened the lips with my fingers, pushing my tongue inside of her. Moving up on the bed between her legs, I pressed the head of my cock against her. She seemed dry or tight and I couldn't get into her easily.

"Do you have something to use on us?" she asked. I said no. She said, "You can put some of my spit on your cock—I will wet it—" and she partly sat up, reaching down for my cock. She took it into her mouth loosely, wetting it. Her saliva dripped from my cock as I edged back down and slid it into her. Once inside of her, she rolled with me, guiding me, moving to her side and then taking me onto my back.

Straddled across me, she pumped up and down while I pulled her upper body towards me and sucked on her ringed nipples. She raised off of me before I came and sort of curled on her side, her hand on my cock. She watched her hand and my cock, moving up and down, her face inches from me.

Moments more and I placed my hand on her head and gently pushed her face down. She kissed my cock and opened her mouth, taking it between her lips.

I was just about to come when the phone rang—the shrill jangle reverberating against the black walls.

I grabbed the receiver and said, "What is it?" I could hear voices and cafe noises in the background but no one was saying anything into the phone. A kind of breathing sound. Placing my hand over hers on my cock to keep her hand still, I sat up and asked into the receiver, "Who is it?" There was a pause and then the line went dead.

"Nobody," I said. She was staring at my cock, squeezing it. The head of it grew red and she kept squeezing it. I was swelling up and in a moment I was spurting come over her hand. She lowered her face and licked at the come as it ran over her hand and between her fingers.

I dropped back on the bed, trying to get my arms around her waist but she was pulling away. She got up and bounced about hurriedly, gathering her clothes. "What are you doing?" I asked. "I must go!" she said. "I must hurry to meet the toilet paper photographer!"

"I wish you'd stay," I said.

She looked at me curiously and smiled. "We have just begun to know each other..." She laughed a little. "Maybe you will be so inspired by knowing me that you will write a marvelous *movie* all about me!"

Another bottle of saki saw me through some scenes in the script but it didn't help me sleep. The skylight was partly open and the air was settling down into the room when the phone rang. My skin felt cold and dry like a dead man's.

Divi said, "I want to talk to you, Jake. Are you asleep?"

"No," I said.

She asked if I'd been in Eston's that evening and I said, "No." She wanted to know if Claude had gone to Eston's. I said, "I believe he was there. There's people still down there. Where are you?" I asked.

"I'm not at home," she said. Someone was speaking to her. I recognized the voice of our Japanese co-producer, Hiromi Nakasha. "Will you come meet me for a drink, Jake? I have been on a train for two days."

"Where did you go?" I asked.

"I wanted to be alone," she said. "I'm flying to London tomorrow. Please see me tonight." She'd meet me at the Hotel Concorde La Fayette. I said I loathed the Concorde La Fayette. "Wait for me in the restaurant behind the currency exchange," she said. "I have left Claude. I am divorcing him."

To stay awake I dropped a couple of the amphetamines, one an ephedrine; anxious, nervous stuff. If I drank more it'd round off the sharp edges. I polished off the saki, pulled on the blue blazer and got my raincoat.

I could hear Arabian music in Eston's and Claude and Che Che's voices above the rest. I paused for a moment, then hurried down the stairs, walked to Saint Germain and caught a cab. sitting back and watching the jumping beads of lights.

Visible across Paris, the Concorde La Fayette was an enormous, skinny structure sticking into the sky like a thermos tube. Surrounded with absurdly gaudy cafes and chunks of commercialized gee-gaw, the lobby had the streamlined, junk-desert ambience of the Dallas air terminal.

The indoor restaurant was empty—a wash of plastic tables and umbrellas beneath the ground floor roof. I bought a New York Times, ordered wine, some bread with mustard and sat for perhaps fifteen minutes. Glancing into the lobby past the giant winged victory statue that dominated the marble desert, I saw Divi with Hiromi, a kind of non-smiling Japanese cover girl in twelve-hundred dollar boots. Her face was like a kabuki mask of non-decipherible messages, and her teeth, while ivory white, seemed to run straight across without a curve. Though taller than Juju, her hands were as small, but chunky, the nails like little moons of red. I believed the cheese-fleshed Leefeldt was enamored with her. I'd watched him stare at her with his mouth sagging open like the lid of a suitcase.

"Hiromi," I said, smiling and rising. "Please..." I nodded to Divi. "You're looking remarkably well. Let me get more glasses—"

"No," Hiromi said, holding up her midget hand. "I am not staying, Jake. I want to talk to you only for a moment."

"Certainly," I said. "Won't you sit down?"

She didn't sit down. "It is about Mark Lajos," she said.

"Of course," I said.

"We are concerned about the time that's been lost, Jake. It is creating some difficult problems for us."

"Our final days," I said, "should've come and gone two weeks ago."

"Yes," Hiromi said. "I have just come from a dinner meeting with Mr. Leefeldt and he is most concerned about our next project."

"As a matter of fact, so am I," I said.

"Let me ask you if you believe that Mark is possibly not the right choice for directing in Tokyo. As you know, our Japanese second unit director—"

"Well—excuse me," I interrupted. "I can understand your reservations at this point and I am most sympathetic."

"Apart from myself," the Japanese wonder girl said, "you are the only other person on this enterprise that Mr. Leefeldt feels he

can trust—" she glanced at Divi. "Of course except for Mr. Duval."
Back to me: "It is of *great* concern, Jake, to the financiers in
Tokyo. Every day there is some new kind of mistake. I am out on
a limb with my people."

"The financiers could no doubt rest more assured," I said,
"with the control more comfortably in their own hands, and
certainly with a Japanese director…"

"To be honest with you," Hiromi said, "and it's only fair that
we are honest with one another, they are most unwilling to
underwrite Mark Lajos if Mr. Leefeldt appears unwilling to move
ahead in that direction. It is Mr. Leefeldt's opinion that a Japanese
director would serve the purposes more successfully of all parties
if this joint venture were more equally assumed."

I nodded. Divi was watching me. "All I can say, Hiromi," I said,
"is that *I* am committed to the Japanese project in due course, and
accordingly defer to any decisions made between the godfather
and Tokyo."

Hiromi looked at her platinum watch. "I must leave. Are you
sure you are all right?" she asked Divi.

"I am fine," Divi said. Hiromi reached out her hand and I got
up and took it gently.

"Thank you for your confidence," she said.

"My pleasure," I said, still on my feet as Hiromi walked across
the lobby. I looked at Divi.

"Very diplomatic of you," she said. "Diplomatic of the
godfather to let you pronounce the verdict. As they say at the
American race track, 'scratch' one Hungarian."

"Sixteen days is sixteen days," I said. "Leefeldt's a man who
lives a day at time. He sees each delay as a deliberate theft, and
there's little margin for error."

"Is it because of the drugs, Jake?"

I said, "Mark's got the assistant—Bertrand—pinch hitting while
he hides in that trailer shooting up with Marjorie—"

"—and Claude?" Divi asked. "He's got Claude sucked into it as
well, hasn't he?"

"That's what they do at Eston's," I said. "Every night. For

Mark, it's instant replay of Beverly Hills."

"How bad is it with Claude?" she asked.

"I don't know *bad* it is," I said. "It's Claude's decision what he does or doesn't do. What do you care anyway?" I poured a glass of wine for her. "You've left him." She was just staring at me, her eyes distant and tearful.

"It is all so hopeless," she said. I reached across and placed my hand on hers. Below the fox collar on the sweater, her blouse was opened, showing her cleavage as a deep shadow with a gold crucifix embedded feet first into the crevice—Christ's head and arms were visible between her breasts. The gold chain glittered as she moved her shoulders and rounded her upper lip over the edge of the glass. She said, "Why did you marry Ann?"

I said. "Why did you marry Claude?"

She didn't say anything. "I feel for the little girl," she said. "For your step-daughter. Was she promiscuous, Jake? Does she understand what is happening?"

"Probably," I said. "I'd been married a year when the kid told me her father, dear old Burt, used to twiddle his finger—that was her word—*twiddle*, between her legs before she started school. I asked her if she'd told her mother this. She shook her head like something out of Our Gang. At twelve years old she said she could talk to me because I wasn't her real father and I'd be a friend to her. She said she wanted to have sex with a man. She said she had dreams every night about a man lying on top of her.

I told her to stop coming in my room. "She reeked of trouble— half-brained," I said. "I mean *slow*. She tried to drive the car. It's not that she didn't know *how* to drive, but that it couldn't occur to her that one had to have some idea of operating one before taking off. She ran though a wall... That's when they diagnosed her as having some head problems.

"And slow in other ways—enticing. Making eyes at actors in and out of the house and even a couple of bimbos Mark'd drag around. But talk about slow-thinkers, take me for example. Mark and Ann'd been carrying on behind my back for half a year, and even that'd bit the dust. Not hard to figure when you consider

Ann and I led pretty separate lives. Separate business—separate rooms."

Divi asked, "Do *you* think Mark did something to the girl that night or is she lying so Ann can get even with Mark and you?"

"We'd been around the pool," I said, "doing coke. The kid was bopping up and down in her bikini and Mark was horsing around, pushing her in the water. I'd gone back in the house when Ann started yelling in the pool house. Mark's lawyer said nothing happened except the kid kept egging him on. He said the girl showed him her tits and wanted to know if they were as good as her mom's. She'd seen Mark and Ann making it a couple of times—she'd snuck up on them. The cops had a field day with the dope, but Mark was out of jail the next day. Big bail. Big time. The press had a ball and Ann managed to dig up a witness—*Nick*, who wasn't even near the pool house. I got it straight from the lawyer that if Nick didn't stick to Ann, she'd hang him on a molestation charge—Mark *and* Nick—like the beans were out of the can and up for grabs."

"That's disgusting," Divi said.

"No," I said. "It's only expedient. Disgusting's not a Hollywood word. Mark's cast as the dirty pipsqueak in the drama and he'll pay the price."

"He *is* a dirty pipsqueak," she said.

"But he is also a talented film maker before we got hold of him. So Nick's in line with Ann. He cleared himself of dope and contributing to the kid's delinquency. Here's a kid meanwhile who's nicking herself with blades that could lead to some serious self-cutting or suicide. Half the time she was so sedated she was like a zombie. In fact, I got the idea for this picture from watching the kid move through a room without touching the floor."

"What's happened to her?" Divi asked.

"My lawyer says she's in a special school somewhere. On ice for kangaroo court. The doctor claims she's had sex and Mark's number one candidate. Ann's got some political hotdog to prove the rape by Mark who wasn't a citizen—never took his citizenship."

We sat drinking the wine, and Divi said, "So here you are, Jake, once again in Paris..."

"The gestapo and the nun," I said.

"I'm not going back to Claude," she said. "Could you ever go back to Ann?"

"The thought of even seeing her horrifies me," I said. "She's got a gun to my head and I'm praying it backfires."

"Would you come to London if I find a movie and we can work together?" she asked.

"Maybe," I said. "Has your holing up with Tokyo Rose got anything to do with a picture in London?"

"Perhaps," she said. "I need her confidence. I need to do something. If I don't have a life I will go insane. Living with Claude has made me crazy. It has taken away my life. I lived only inside of him. Now he's lost." I shrugged. She said, "Can I help him?"

"No," I said.

She sighed and drank. "I hate him," she said. I drank. "What do you feel about Ann?" she asked. "Anger? Hatred?"

"I don't feel anything," I said. "That's how I feel about everything."

"What do you feel about me?" she asked.

"What do you want me to feel?"

"Drawn to me—attracted to me—"

"I am attracted to you," I said. "I'm not drawn to you—" I signaled the waiter. He came. I was instructing him to bring another better bottle with two fresh glasses when Divi placed her hand on my arm.

"Come up with me," she said. "I am staying here in the hotel." I canceled the order and paid the check. Divi snuggled her arm into mine, then pulled away and stepped back. "Life is monstrous," she said.

"Because we're monsters," I said.

We rode the elevator to the thirty-third floor like a cushioned bullet. At the top, I could hear pounding. Half the floor seemed under construction. Inside the long thin room I went to the window and stared down at Paris, the tips of my toes against the glass as though there was no separation from the blank space. I saw myself falling through the glass, toppling downwards to that black ribbon of busy boulevard. "May I draw the drape?" I asked.

"I like it open," she said. "Turn off the overhead light."

"The sky reflects the glow into the room." I turned the switch off and the walls took a muted blue glow. She brought out a bottle of bourbon and two glasses. "I want to get drunk," she said. She looked slightly shaky. I asked if she was cold. "No," she said. "I am hot and afraid." She got back up to break out the small ice tray. "I asked them for a bucket," she said. "There is no bucket."

"I can get drunk without it," I said.

"Yes," she said, dropping ice cubes into our glasses and filling them with bourbon. "You felt something for me three years ago, didn't you, Jake?"

"Yes," I said. "You were kooky. You knocked me out."

"Do you think it is some bizarre astrological kink or bend in our personalities that we have done such funny things?" I said I didn't know. "What did you feel for me?" she asked.

I sat back. "I remember the cafe—"

"De la Gare," she said. "It was cold."

"The glass partitions were around the tables," I said. "You were peering through one of the panes."

"They said I would find you there. I didn't see you and called—"

"I knocked on the glass with the tip of my pen."

"Grosse noir," she said. "Are you surprised I remember that?"

"Yes," I said. "I still use a broad point. Black ink."

"I remember everything," she said.

We sat and drank, Divi drinking to get drunk. I didn't think I could get drunk.

I said, "I don't remember most things well anymore. I have fleeting images—disconnected pictures."

"If it were possible for you and I to find something together—" she said but then stopped. She drank what was in her glass. "If you cared for me now I probably would not go to London tomorrow."

I couldn't sense anything between Divi and myself. I only felt somewhat sick to my stomach. Maybe the pills. I felt drained like a man who'd taken a beating big at some gamble and sat unsure of what he'd lost. Such a man dies quickly.

Divi refilled my glass and topped off hers. She was watching me, waiting for me to say something. She picked up the glass and tipped it to her lips, almost emptying it. She stretched, reaching her hands towards the low ceiling. Her black arms were beautiful. We were in a blue box with one edge open to an enormous fall. She lowered her arms and stared at me. It was as though we were looking at each other across some incredible gap—a hole in the earth. She was on a ship passing an island of the dead. I was on the sands and not even waving as the ship sailed past.

She said, "God, I feel ill..."

We finished the sewer shots the following days during a freak hot spell. Only half the crew stayed into the night. Bertrand had been set by the godfather to wrap *Sucant Le Sang* during Mark's so-called sudden illness. Eston said, "It's actually his fucking kidneys. Mark's so totally pumped full of shit and medication he's turning green."

Unofficially, both Mark and Marjorie were off at a Hungarian journalist's hotel party, and by late afternoon we were close to the end of the picture. Two more shots of Juju in her panties running underground to escape the vampire, finished her on the picture. Bertrand kept close on her, a lot of extra coverage and reaction shots than Mark would've scheduled. When we broke for a very late lunch, she was jabbering with Robert and I took her aside. "Juju," I said, "you looked sensational. When this damn picture's released they'll be hollering for you all over town."

"Maybe somebody will holler for me to go to L.A.!" she said. "And because you have helped me, Jake. Because I would not have oral sex with Mark Lajos I knew he would not treat me very well. I am glad you are here."

"You never told me that about Mark—" I said.

"Robert warned me if I caused trouble I might not work in this movie. He also said Mark could get into trouble with the godfather."

"He's already in trouble with the godfather," I said. "Will I see you later?"

"I will be at the Red Egg with Robert, Jake. We will celebrate and go dancing and see Tanyous playing in the band. You can come and *dance* with me!"

I said we had a couple more setups, but I'd see her before she took off.

After Bertrand made some last shots, we broke and I looked for Juju but she'd disappeared. Robert had gone back to the offices and I figured she'd ridden with him. Claude corrected me.

"One of those Iranians showed up on a motorcycle and she left with him," he said. He looked ludicrous—an old witch with plastic fangs and a ratty wig. His gum infection had swollen the right side of his face.

It was dark and the heat in the sewers was bearing down when we grabbed Claude's last shot in two takes, marking the end of the filming. No one was happy. Still in makeup minus the fangs, Claude was hurrying off for an emergency meeting with his dentist. Eston, grumbling over the stills, told him we'd probably be at Cafe Leper.

Shutting down was a lot of empty motions, almost amateurish, and nobody'd made plans about a party. One of the bit players reminded us that it was bad luck to wrap without a celebration, so after a quick huddle and despite the heat, a couple of actors and Bertrand, along with his assistant, joined Eston and myself at Montmarte bar.

The music was loud and over drinks I told Eston what Juju'd said about Mark. "I've hooked the bastard up with a few other little twerps thinking they're going to get themselves in the movies," he said. "He gets them copping his dick once or twice and forgets who they are. That's what the son of a bitch is like.

But he didn't get to *her* because he's afraid of Leefeldt, and Juju didn't come by way of Mark—or me, for that matter."

Another round and Bertrand caught some Chinese tourists. One of the actors said, "He can speak some Chinese..." So we sat in the dull loud bar listening to Bertrand repeat a Chinese joke which the orientals didn't seem to understand. Eston leaned against me and said, "What's the deal with you and Divi?"

"She left for London," I said. "She told me she was getting a divorce."

"Well, that's off," Eston said. "Marjorie told me Divi isn't going to divorce Claude even though his prick's so small she said she can't feel it fucking her. Claude's just got another picture because of this cinematic atrocity," he said. "Keep it under your hat—he's trying to keep it a secret until he's signed the deal. But Marjorie talked to Divi who thinks he's going to score some big bucks so she says she's going to hang in. She's had some guy who runs a joint on Clerkenwell and she was singing there last Fall. Old chanteuse sort of shit, Jake. You'd love it."

"She was actually singing?" I said.

"Yeah, and a few dumps here. Billie Holiday stuff—blues stuff. She isn't half bad when she's all decked out in a sequined dress that's cut down to her snatch practically." He smiled. "But you know all that, don't you?" I didn't say I didn't. "You were getting a little since you got here, weren't you, Jake?" I just looked at him. "It's okay," he said. "Claude's been thinking she's off with you again but since she's gone over there he doesn't know what to think. I mean if you consider he ever knew what to think to start with. Listen, Jake—" he said confidentially. "Talking about chic dresses, Che Che's got this silver number that's opened down the back. I mean, so while Divi's off in London now singing to the Brits, a little moonlighting's going on in Claude's backyard."

"You saying he's got something going with *Che* Che?" I said.

"It's a blast," Eston said. "They get dancing and hugging and pretty soon they snoozy off into the bedroom. I think half the time they're so smashed they don't know what they're doing, but on the other hand he's turning queer right in front of our eyes.

Like tonight," he said, "Paul's bringing some shit that's just out of Morocco. It's supposed to be the finest quality in the fucking world, Jake. He's also got a gal who's from the Zanzibar or somewhere—black as night, man, and tall as a goddamn Amazon. Taller than you or me, Jake. She makes Divi look like a *white* man! Only speaks Swahili. You know Paul can speak Swahili?"

"I had no idea," I said. "I didn't know Bertrand speaks Chinese."

"That's *not* Chinese," he said. "He can't speak Chinese any more than I can speak Swahili. So this amazon's brought the shit in, Jake." He leaned closer. "Paul's got a deal with Mark about this new stuff, and Mark's got a cowboy singer coming over—what the fuck's his name? He was running around after Willie Nelson for a while. He's part of the deal. You got to come down, Jake. This'll be the fucking party!"

I said I didn't know—I wasn't sure what I was doing.

"You've got the shut-down blues," he said. "If we were back home in the States we'd be partying up a sound stage instead of sneaking off like we're some kind of thieves. But, hey, neighbor, all you got to do now is walk downstairs."

We headed for Cafe Leper for another round, leaving Bertrand and one of the actors behind with the Chinese. The rest of us piled into a cab. His face inches from mine, Eston said, "Everyone's talking about you scoring with the little chick, Jake. I mean you've been *scoring*, right?" He didn't seem to care if I said something or not. "Just wondering how long she's going to ride you—" he said.

"What do you mean 'ride' me?" I said.

"The girl's this opportunist, mystery chick who works people. She worked me—"

"She said you haven't paid her—"

"I will!" he said.

"Question of who rides who," I said, "like the saying goes." In Cafe Leper, Sonia was making all kinds of signals. The law'd been in and was hanging around. "They are no good bastards," she said, giving me another drink. "Leaning on my ass because they aren't getting enough!"

I bought drinks for the three glum-faced dwarfs at the bar while Eston talked to an old German he knew from some documentary. The guy as pale and pasty as a bunch of squeezed-together paper towels. Sonia'd told me he was an ex-Nazi agent. I'd never seen him talking in the bar to anyone but Eston.

Phillipe was wearing his huge baseball mits, and sipping wine through a plastic straw. The next round I switched to vodka and had it poured for the dwarfs.

Staying on my stool at the end of the bar, I was hoping Juju'd come bouncing down the steps. Maybe another half-hour of meaningless movie talk with the actor—all the while wondering why I was waiting for a neurotic teenager on rollerblades. Looking at myself in any mirror I could see the reason. Behind the dead face I was getting desperate. An over-the-hill Hollywood hack on the chase, and the girl knew I was chasing. That was the screwy link in the dumb puzzle.

Phillipe was telling me about the Spaniard with the biggest cock of the dwarfs when Claude showed up with gauze in his mouth. We all laughed at him. "The vampire!" Eston joked. "Get a bite of a bad one?" Claude looked red—almost sunburned. The makeup was gone except around his neck and he squeezed between Phillipe and myself, staring at me in a weird way. Pulling the gauze from his mouth. "So another one's down, eh, Jake?" he said. "One more for you to chalk off. Right, Jake?"

I said he was right. He looked in pain and Eston passed a handful of pills into Claude's palm that quickly went into the still-bleeding mouth. I said, "Why don't you go home, Claude? You're a movie star. You need to bask in your celebrity."

He shook his head. "With Divi working in London there is nothing at home. If I go there I might burn the place down. I will start fire to the furniture." He turned to Eston. "If we're going, let's *go*! Or maybe you're going to the *ballet*—" he said to me. "Are you going to the bal*let*, Jake?"

"Okay, Claude, I'll bite," I said. "What's at the fucking ballet?"

"Art!" he said.

"Art *who?*" Phillipe said. We laughed again.

Claude said, "You need to talk to me about Divi, Jake. She said she talked to you about getting a divorce."

"Sketchily," I said. "I told her it was dangerous territory, and I wasn't the one to talk about divorce."

"So what did you talk about with my Divi?" he asked.

"Oh, Claude..." I said. "We had so little to talk about."

"But once upon a time you seemed to have plenty to talk about," he said.

"Once upon a time," I said, "is once upon a time, Claude. God created the past so us humans could have wastebaskets."

I stayed behind, watching them crowd the stairs behind Eston like the Three Stooges, Claude's ass almost twice as wide as on his last picture. He needed a psychiatrist.

Feeling unsteady and shaky, I knew I'd have to eat or I'd keel over. Phillipe's face was close to mine and his breathe was like a mackerel. He was whispering about Claude but I couldn't tell what he was saying. I looked around the Cafe Leper—a good name for the place; a couple other rotten Americans like myself at the bar, the forgotten Nazi'd drifted into the shadows while some sleazy French grifters argued over a card deck. The dwarfs were drinking side by side like a row of salt and pepper shakers. There was a pair of old hookers at a table, one tall and all lower end like a kangaroo, eyeballing Sonia's greaseball bouncer who sat like a junkyard dog watching everyone else.

The girl wasn't coming, and I took maybe another half-hour to empty the drink. I pictured her romping with the Arabs or Iranians who looked so freshly stretched out of puberty.

Slipping on the steps as I left the cafe, I had to check myself— I was drifting inside myself again—something like someone coming loose from within my own skin and shaking around, jarring against the walls of myself.

Minutes later I was in a cab heading to rue Serpante. The taxi inched through traffic at a snail's pace, and the dirty windshield reflected the lights like slow-pulsing bleeps or spectacular bugs squashed under pieces of glass. The heat was worse. I had to get out of the cab, and as I stared across Saint Germain to rue Hautefeuille, a familiar voice called to me.

Samson Sechan was waving that ivory cigarette holder—half serpent and naked concubine, now yellowing with age. A wide brimmed red hat was cocked rakishly to one side of his head, shadowing his face. But the lights of the cars skimmed over the nests of lines circling his eyes and stretching down his thin, wrinkled neck.

Blowing a cloud of smoke, he smiled and reached his other hand for mine. "My *god*," he said, "I'm so pleased to see you, Jake!" The hair at his temples and mustache was dyed a peculiar dark color that pallored his face.

"Sam, you look wonderful!" I said, holding his hand.

"You've never come to see me!" he said. "I've been hurt terribly, Jake. But I understand and I forgive you."

"It's been this movie. We finished the damn thing a few hours ago."

"*I* should've played the vampire, you know," he said. "Duval's so impossibly pathetic—he's like a fat butcher. I procrastinated, Jake, I actually procrastinated and your producer—who incidentally is a dear friend—"

"I know," I said.

"He be*seech*ed me to play the vampire *ages* ago!"

"It's been one of his dreams," I said. "A vampire in the sewers of Paris."

"But he im*plored* me to consider the role, and I even *read* for that dreadful little Hungarian. His first two pictures were *mar*velous, Jake! How can one forget?"

"It's easy," I said.

"Yes, it is—it is. He's lost the thread com*plet*ely, hasn't he? And with an attitude that's distanced everyone once supportive of him. He's a rotten little fascist, isn't he, Jake?"

"This'll be an awful movie," I said. "The whole thing's been a jumbled nightmare. I hate making movies."

"You're crying in your champagne, Jake. From the horses mouth, I know your salary's breaking the bank at Monte Carlo!"

"Very funny, Sam—"

"Though you've neglected me, I've followed your career *scrupu*lously, I might add. My little pipeline has told me you're contracted on the Japa*nese* movie these little yellow people have trapped the French into joining—" He flagged the waiter with his cigarette holder and asked for more wine and another glass. "As they said on the television, Jake, you've got the Midas touch."

"Instead of gold," I said, "it turns into cheese."

"You re*do* cheese from nothing into something the mass can assimilate—that unwashed, grotesque mass. Mind you, you've an incredible talent, Jake, but I'm perpetually surprised you're not pro*du*cing. Is it still that you're unwilling to lay aside the ridiculous gauntlet you keep throwing down in the name of art?" I shook my head, smiling, but he said, "No, no, my boy, you *do* and it's so terribly obvious to us who only salute you—who have nothing left! I mean *serious*ly—look at this kisser! What more hideous a vampire could one imagine? Little children run at the sight of me. They cry out and flee to the arms of their mothers. I see horror in their eyes. Jake, I can't even get a decent blowjob!"

I stared at him and started to laugh. We both laughed. "I was wonderful, wasn't I, Jake? Could anyone imagine how many lovely women I murdered? Ten thousand?"

"That many?" I said.

"It had to be, wouldn't you say? How many years? You were a *boy*, Jake—a lovely boy and so filled with wonder! My god, you were a child no older than your step-daughter—"

"Ex-step daughter," I said. The skin on Samson's face was so fragile the thin blue veins appeared to be moving beneath it. "Eston Sthole said you knew the artist Jean Paul Vermond?"

"The one that committed suicide," he said. "It was in all the news. *Paris Confidential* did a show about it—some sort of question about the suicide. The family wasn't convinced because of that girl."

"The one in the movie," I said.

"Yes," he said.

"What do you know about Vermond?" I asked. "Maybe a

movie in it."

"But will *I* be in the movie?" he said. "That's the only question that matters, Jake!"

"Of course you'll be in it," I said. "Only an idea I'm playing with—"

"I'm teasing you, my boy."

"If I say so you'll be in it, Sam."

"You have that power now, don't you? I'm very impressed, Jake." He raised his glass. I raised mine. We drank. "The Vermonds, you know, they're Cherbourg people. Dreadful people tied into shipping and what used to some Norwegian steamship line. A remarkably talented fellow, Jean Paul. His shows were wonderful—very Robert Mapplethorpe—though Vermond wasn't gay that anyone *knows* about..."

"What was it about the suicide that's questionable?" I asked.

"His feet," Samson said. "They were on the floor, I believe. He'd hanged himself but somehow the rope had slipped or some such thing following his death. It's one of these little French dramas the police so enthusiastically puzzle over."

"What about the girl?" I asked.

"One of chorus line, Jake. I was at an opening a year ago, and he'd sold this Marilyn Monroe piece to the museum. A life sized plaster stature he'd used the girl for—plastering over her, or whatever he did. Supposedly he sold the piece for an enormous amount, and that's where this mystery comes in because there was some sort of robbery involved—least that's the notion that's been entertained..." He sipped his wine delicately. "I'm having a party, Jake, on the next full moon and I insist that you be there. You can get your ears filled with the gossip. Your producer will be there, who sincerely is a dear friend, unlike that little Hungarian and that Miss Acne he's sporting. Leefeldt actually re*quested me* to be the vampire! He implored me to work in the film—can you believe it? I read for the motherfuckers—*me, Sam*son Se*chan*! I never do readings for these faggots and fuckers!"

"I would've liked working with you again, Sam."

"That's why you must become a pro*d*u*c*er, Jake. You must throw away your notions of beatnik glory and *face* reality! The girl must be screwing the little fascist to be working in the picture."

"She was actually brought in by Robert Kamp—"

"He's a lovely boy, Jake. We're close, Robert and I. Of course, she was in the news because of Vermond's suicide and Robert—though I love him—is such a pack-rat with all these modicums of celebrity, though mind you she was no more than a pit in the prune. The core of Vermond's Marilyn Monroe piece, I mean. The girl was simply the inner thing he plastered over!"

Ashes fell from his cigarette. "All of this makes absolute sense but I can't *fathom* what's in the minds of these young people," he said. "I simply can't, Jake. But then I can't fathom what's happened to this city. It's disgusting. It's repulsive. I'm moving to Spain."

"You'll never leave Paris," I said.

"Oh, I will! I'll sell my flat and retire. But who'll be looking for me? How hideous it all is—" He glanced at his watch. "I'm late for my yoga. It's my back. My spine—" He emptied his glass and stood up. "You'd better be good, Jake. You'd better call me."

I said I would and he walked away, sprightly, like a man thirty years younger than he was. He'd made his laugh the most satanical I'd ever heard. He'd hiss like a giant snake; some trick with his diaphragm and front teeth. He was an incredible American exile that'd never gone. Years ago he'd told me his drunken father'd pushed a flashlight up into Sam's ass when he was nine years old and he'd almost bled to death.

The day his father died in a field in Kansas, Sam ran away from the body. He told no one where it was. When found, the crows had eaten the eyeballs out and mouth off the face.

No air in the dim hall, The walls felt hot and moist like the intestines of an animal. Passing Eston's door, I could hear Mark's bitching–whining, the thudding music and Marjorie laughing hysterically. Almost on tip toes, I snuck beyond his darkroom door, around the corner and up the last sewer-like steps.

As I came up into the glow from the dull yellow light over the door, I found a bare foot sticking over the edge of the top stair.

Juju was in front of my door, curled fetus-like with one leg stretching back. The black panties showed at the opened seat of the black leather chaps, low on her waist and buckled at the small of her back facing me. Her other leg was tucked beneath her, the soles of both bare feet nearly black from the stairs, halls, and no doubt the streets of Paris.

I took hold of her ankle and shook her, rousing her a little, then sort of brought her up onto her feet. "Jake..." she said without opening her eyes. "I want to stay with you–"

I unlocked the door. "Where are your skates?" I asked.

She shook her head. She didn't know. Tipping onto the bed face down, she crawled up lengthwise a little, her black-soled feet hanging over the edge.

I don't remember pushing her over so I could get into the bed, but I woke up with a jolt–as though I'd been tapped with an electric wire. It was dark, the sky was starless, like a black pool and my throat was on fire. The heat was pressing as though the ceiling had sunk down. I brought my legs off the bed, opened a bottle of water and drank, then took off my socks and shirt.

Juju lay bundled in with the blanket and leopard skin sheet, breathing shallowly. She didn't even seem conscious. Her pulse was racing and she rolled onto her back, the cover falling off the other side of the bed. Raising her arms above her head, one hand groped between the bars of the head rail. Her nipples were sticking up and I lifted the sheet from her sweating stomach and stared at the moon light showing white on her body. I couldn't remember her taking off the tee-shirt or leather chaps that were on the floor on my side of the bed. She'd taken the ring out of her navel.

I touched her belly button, put the tip of my finger into it. She didn't wake but turned her face toward me. Her hair was growing in on the sides above her ears. Long pale orange eyelashes. I touched her neck and then her lips. She opened her mouth slightly and I felt her teeth, then pushed two fingers into her mouth, feeling her tongue. She curled towards me, taking hold of my wrist and started sucking on my fingers.

My cock sprung up and I pushed the sheet aside. Taking hold of myself, swollen and hot, I reached to her head, pulled her face down, turning her on the bed and putting my cock against her mouth.

She made a choking sound as I shoved between her lips and far in until I felt the back of her throat. She started gagging. Holding her head with both hands, I fucked her in the mouth. Several deep thrusts and I was coming. She choked and coughed but I kept my cock in her mouth. After a few moments I drew back, pulling it out, and her hand flopped around my stomach, reaching across me. I bent over to the floor and got the wine bottle and then held her head up again as I tipped its mouth to her lips. She drank—coughed, swallowed more and dropped back onto the mattress.

There was no sleep in the heat. The skylight cracked open a foot alleviated some, but jammed the noises into the space. Juju's body was on fire each time she came close to me, or rolled around, her ass burning to the touch. Yet the small of her back was cool. I edged her over. She wasn't waking up. Mumbling something, she threw her right leg on top of me.

"Juju," I said. "Juju! Wake up or move over for god's sake." I was split in two with exhaustion. The noise from Eston's, rolling through his floor earlier, had faded. I'd heard a shriek before I'd fallen into a troubled sleep. Laughing. They were crazy. I envied Eston's deaf mother.

I wanted another drink and let my left arm drop towards the floor for the bottle. Shaking Juju, I said, "Do you want a drink of something?"

She muttered, "I am still swallowing your come..."

I reached over her and pulled the blanket back up on the bed, tucking it about her body. She looked so small. Like a little package. I could not wake her again and lay there staring at the dark sky through the partly opened skylight. The heat had lifted and I was sinking into sleep with just the leopard sheet over me. The sky was like ink. Some angle of looking at it from where I was on the bed, so that the reflections of the city dimmed. I was asking myself how could that be? What was I dreaming? *Was* I dreaming?

It took me moments to realize someone was at my door. They were right outside the door, rapping on it—saying something. It sounded like Marjorie.

I grabbed the sheet up as I climbed off the bed, slung it around myself and walked to the door, a friendly walk crossing the Persian carpets and that soft worn wood. I opened the door. Marjorie was standing there sort of swaying one way and then the other in some slow circular motion. She didn't know she was doing it. "Jake," she said, "I'm scared. I'm actually scared to fucking death."

"Amazing," I said, clearing my throat. "What are you scared of, Marjorie?"

"Can I come in?"

I stepped back. "I'm not alone," I said.

She sort of drifted in. "It's so dark," she said, leaning forward from the waist.

"I was asleep. The walls are black—"

"He's in the bloody can—"

"Who's in the can?"

"Who the fuck else? Mark. Mark the bloody fuck head.."

"So?"

"He's shot up again, Jake, on top of what he's already shot up and he's in there by himself now. Paul's gone. Eston had him take away all the goddamn dope. They had a row. Goddamn row."

"I thought I heard a lot of noise," I said. "So what's it got to do with me?"

She was squinting at me. "What're you fucking wearing? A leopard skin toga?"

"It's a sheet, Marjorie. You got me out of bed. What time is it?"

"Who *knows*, Jake. You want to come and talk him out of the can? He won't answer and nobody can talk him out. Eston won't break the door lock or the bloody door because he's bitching it's a bloody antique—it's like a steel vault for a fucking privy!"

Marjorie's breasts seemed abnormally large and packed. I reached up and put my hand on her breast.

"I'd like to get him out of the fucking bathroom," she said. "I don't mind coming up because I'm going to split, you know. I'm going to get out of here tonight—"

"I have those feelings myself—"

She tried to look past me but couldn't see anything. She whispered, "Did you boff me last week after I did the fisting?" I shrugged. "I thought I was dreaming, Jake. Mark said he thought you boffed me off, but I said I couldn't remember a bloody second of it." She squinted past me into the dark room. "That's the little tart, isn't it? You've been seeing that little kid, haven't you?"

I said, "What do you want me to do, Marjorie?" Her breast was beating like a heart in my palm.

"I'll come back up sometime when we get the damned fool out of the can, Jake. I get all scared with someone in a bloody can not answering when you holler at the door."

"Okay," I said. I threw the sheet on the bed and got my pants. Again she whispered, "You've got a lovely backside, Jake. It's truly lovely."

"Thanks," I said. "Your's is okay, too, Margie." I got my pants on, pulled on a shirt and stuck my feet into the shoes. "Let's go see what's up."

"He said if something went sour to come up and fetch you, Jake—"

"Who said that?"

"Eston—"

"I didn't think it'd be Mark. Let's go."

We went downstairs, she going first and I put my hand on the back of her neck. I thought about bringing her back up into bed with Juju and myself. We got down to Eston's and the door was ajar. I went in.

Che Che was on the couch. Eston was sitting in front of the television with headphones on. He looked up and pulled he headphones off. The whites of his eyes were red. "He's in the bathroom doing one of his fucking numbers, Jake. I'm not going to break my goddamn door for one of Mark's numbers."

I knocked on the bathroom door. No answer. "Mark—" I said. "It's me. Open the door so I can go to bed. Eston wants you out of his bathroom." I put my ear to the door. No sound—a dripping noise. "He's left the water on," I said. "What's he doing in there?"

"Getting sick," Che Che said. "He went in sick."

"Shit," I said. "Was he puking?"

"Dry heaves—shocking," Eston said. "He said he was sick."

"We're going to have to open the door."

"I can't—he's got it locked from inside."

"Well, fuck, Eston, I mean we have to open it. He might need help."

"He can say if he needs help," Eston said.

"He can't say it if he's *sick*!" Marjorie said.

"He's probably dead," Che Che said, rolling up off the couch.

I put my shoulder to the door.

"*Don't*!" Eston yelled. "That's door's fragile!"

"Then go out the goddamn window!" I said.

"Not me," he said.

"Che Che—you're acrobatic," Marjorie said. "You climb out the window and open the bloody bathroom window."

"Shit!" Che Che said. "What if I fall?"

"You won't fall," Eston said. "It's a five foot maneuver to the bathroom window. You just reach out and it's there."

"It's *your* window," Che Che said. "Why don't you go out?"

"Simple. Because I'm not a window climber. I'm acrophobic and you're here—obligated to me."

"Oh, so what am I supposed to be? Some fucking cat burglar?"

"Just go out and open the window," I said. "Go in and open the door from inside."

Exasperated, Che Che arranged his clothing, and then went to the living room windows.

Climbing awkwardly, precariously out onto the narrow ledge, Che Che shimmied against the wall the few feet to the bathroom window, still reaching back for Eston's hand. Managing a grip on the bathroom window ledge, Che Che pulled and yanked and said, "I can't open the window! It won't go in—"

"Out! *Out!*" Eston yelled. "Open it *out* and don't break the glass! It's seventeenth *century!*"

Standing at the closed door, I could hear Che Che climbing through the window into the bathroom, the high heels grating on the tile floor. "Yikes!" he said. "Jesus *Christ*—he's on the fucking floor in a mess of his own fucking vomit and he's *cold*—"

Rattling at the door from inside, Che Che got it open and quickly pushed past me, gasping, showing Mark motionless on the tile beside the toilet. Greenish puke had spilled over the bowl and onto the floor. I looked down at him. He was blue. His eyes were partly open. I felt his neck and then his wrist. He was dead.

Quick flashes of light at my back. Eston was in the bathroom taking pictures. The full impact hadn't hit Marjorie and she said, "What're you doing? What's the matter with Mark?" She punched past Eston and stood beside me looking down at him. She gasped and covered her mouth with her hands. "Is he...?"

"Yeah," I said. "He's dead." I looked at Eston focusing and shooting two more shots. "You knew he was dead, didn't you?"

"I figured he was," he said. He looked at me. "I had to get the dope out of the flat, Jake. Paul's gone with it. The police'll be going over the flat with a comb. You got any dope up there?"

"No," I said. "Just pills."

"Well, I don't think they'll go up there to see you, but they'll want to talk about it. I got to call them now. You want to call, Jake?"

"It's your flat, Eston. You call."

"But you found him—" he said.

"No, you call, Eston. Fuck this shit. You've got a corpse in your bathroom—"

Marjorie started crying, grasping at her stomach and her face.

"Okay, okay—" Eston said, "I'll call. Tell them just like it is—he went in there and we didn't know what he was doing."

"I'll call!" Che Che said. "I like to call authorities—"

"Jesus—Jesus," Marjorie was saying.

"Leave me the fuck out of it," I said. "Come out of there," I told Marjorie, taking her by the arm, pulling her. "Come out and sit down." Che Che was on the phone.

"Don't tell them who he is," I said. "You'll have the press here. You better call Leefeldt in New York," I told Eston, "as soon as he gets off the phone. Let the godfather handle the bullshit."

"You're right, Jake," Eston said, nervous now, scampering about to tidy the apartment. He looked at Marjorie. "You better get out of here, Margie. Go on with Jake."

"No, I'm not going," she said. "I'm not leaving Mark like this—"

"He's not interested anymore, girl," Che Che said, one hand over the phone.

"There's nothing you can do, Marjorie," I said. "The press'll be all over you—"

"So let them!" she said. "I'm not leaving him like this."

Eston winked at me, saying to Marjorie, "You're going to be on Paris Confidential tomorrow night!"

"I don't care," she said.

"You *do* care, honey," Che Che said, "it's the reason you're staying!"

"Shut up!" Marjorie said. "Get me a goddamn drink." Eston started into the kitchen.

"Are you staying, Jake?" he asked.

I shook my head. "I'm going back to bed. Tell them the story and leave me out of it. She didn't come up and get me."

"He's got the little kid in bed with him," Marjorie said. "The jujube girl."

"They'll want to talk to you anyway," Eston said.

I walked out into the hall, Eston behind me. He whispered, "I got some good shots, Jake. Paparazzi's going to eat their fucking hearts out!"

Three days later. I felt okay about Mark meeting his maker. I knew the godfather'd share similar sentiments and promote the hell out of the picture. He'd made three hundred calls and was on his way to New York via the Concorde. In all ways, it was a good thing that'd happened.

But I felt haunted. Something breathing on my neck. Maybe guilt because I wasn't unhappy that Mark was dead. Yet some foreboding seemed to be hanging—a cloud like in the funny books where a black balloon floats over someone's head.

Things I could ascertain immediately seemed meaningless. The Japanese script seemed meaningless. Trite, no worse than trite. Rotten, even though Hiromi said they loved what I'd overnighted to Tokyo. They wanted to know when I'd finish it and I didn't have an answer.

I couldn't tell what was wrong. I kept thinking it was the combination again, the pills and alcohol. Eston and I shared a bottle of wine in plastic cups with ice cubes while we wound up the stills. Several shots of Juju in her pink panties, one of her red towel flapping behind as she raced through the sewers—the vampire supposedly close at her hind-end. The waving flag of red looked like a mid-air splash of blood. We had Claude's double make the sewer run for the vampire because Robert said our star was "prostrate with grief..."

Not so Marjorie. We got her screaming wildly with her tits hanging out. She milked Mark's departure as a personal inconvenience while weeping for the cameras, claiming Mark had proposed marriage. She was leaving for Budapest the following day, accompanying Mark's return to his native soil.

Jacques Cardiff was beside himself and blew the thirty minute show into sixty for the occasion. I refused to be interviewed though they ran the clips from the show I'd done.

I didn't know whether it was Saturday or Sunday but could hear Juju whispering. I couldn't open my eyes but pictured the hushed words as hairy lumps rising and falling as they moved in a line like caterpillars. When I did open my eyes the bright sun was coming through the skylight. The flat black walls looked gray, somehow illuminated.

Juju was in the chair to the left of the bed and quickly reaching to hang up the phone. Slumping down in my shirt, opened down the front of her breasts, her panties creased deeply between her legs. She had the Luger pistol in her lap. Glancing down at it, she said, "Do you think Mark Lajos killed himself with the dope?"

"I don't know," I said.

She picked up the gun. "Is this loaded?" she asked, turning it upside down and staring into the empty chamber for the magazine. "This is a hole where the bullets go in?"

I nodded. "There's a clip for it. You load the clip and slide it inside the grip—the handle. It's a relic—very old, but valuable as Luger's go."

"I want to hold it," she said. "But maybe there is bullets inside of it?"

"I've already tested that," I said.

"If you give me the bullets I will put them in and shoot it!" she said.

"Who would you shoot?"

"Oh, I would shoot it through the glass in the roof. I would shoot these people I do not like! Have you ever shot someone with this gun, Jake?" She got up from the chair and came to the bed, plopped down beside me and held the gun in both hands.

"Yes," I said.

"Who did you shoot?" she asked.

"A Russian," I said.

"Was he a spy?"

"No," I said. "He was a movie extra."

"Did he die from being shot?"

"No," I said. "It was an accident and he sued the studio."

"He didn't get shot in the heart?"

I said, "He got shot in the groin and bled like a pig."

She held the gun close to her face, looking at it. "How would you have felt if he had died?"

"I wouldn't have cared one way or the other," I said. "I never liked him."

She laughed. "That is how I feel sometimes," she said, lifting the gun up and down. "It is a heavy gun..."

"Good metal back in the pre-war days," I said.

"What would you do to shoot yourself with it?" she asked, nudging the barrel against her cheek. "People put it in their mouth."

"Yes," I said. "They put it all kinds of places."

"Can I shoot it?" she asked.

"Shoot it?"

"Pull the trigger..." she said.

"Go ahead. You have to slide the upper part back until it stops. It'll stay. Now it's ready to fire."

"Where should I shoot it?" she asked. "Do I just pull the trigger?"

"You squeeze it," I said. "Put your finger through the guard— your thumb on the other side. That's where it belongs. Now you just squeeze it like a ball."

"The little part will fly down and *bang*!" she said.

"And it'll be ready to fire again—"

"Can I shoot you with it?" she asked.

"Me?"

Her eyes were bright, her upper lip lifting slightly with an excited breath. She lowered the barrel and placed the muzzle against my chest. "You're sure there are no bullets in the gun?" she asked.

"Well," I said, "I can't imagine there are but we can give it a try."

Her whole face showed a cautious, determined squeeze. It was harder than she thought. She made a slight grimace and the hammer snapped. She jerked back, stunned and surprised.

"That's it?" she said. "If there had been a bullet in it, I would have shot you."

"That's right," I said.

"There would be a lot of blood."

"Probably."

"This is exciting!" she said. "Can I shoot you again?"

"Go ahead," I said. Her tongue pushed between her lips. I wanted to bite on it. The left four fingers closed over the right fingers curled on the grip. Her first finger tightened on the trigger. Again the snap—startling her, the muzzle jumping back slightly, then forward with her surprise, jarring against my rib.

"I am sorry!" she said, then laughed dazedly. "I must be crazy! This is a *real* gun—my god!" She dropped the Luger against my leg. "Give me your hand," she said. Taking my wrist, she placed my fingers between her legs. "Maybe you could shoot *me* in the groin—would I bleed like a pig?"

"You'd bleed like a lamb..." I said.

"Would you like to see me bleed like an animal?"

"Yes," I said, staring at her wondrous face.

"Maybe—maybe I will bleed if this goes inside of me..." She was pushing the muzzle against the panties covering her sex, pushing the barrel between my hand and her crotch. "I want you to stick it inside of me—" I could feel her heat and wetness. The pressure of her pelvis edged against my hand and I slid my fingers under the panties along the moist lips. Her eyes were wide and she drew her breath as I turned the gun around—the muzzle against her.

"Like this?" I asked.

She seemed flustered for a moment, pulled her panties down off one leg and pushed my hand with both of hers, the barrel pointing down but upwards into her crotch. Staring at me intensely and holding my wrist, she moved the barrel back and forth and sideways, working it into herself.

In a moment she said, "It is in*side* of me!" She pulled hard on my wrist, sliding the barrel into herself. "Ohhh!" she cried painfully. "You do it! You do it!" she said, gasping. "Fuck me with it!" She let go of my wrist and wrapped her arms around my neck. I pushed the gun into her, then drew it out slowly, then pressed it into her again. "All the way!" she said.

"It's all the way," I said. The trigger guard was knocking against her public bone. I could feel her muscles tightening, stretching, the tender skin giving back to the steel. "Shoot it!" she cried. "Shoot it in me!"

I pulled the trigger—once—then again. Snap! Snap!

"Yes!" she gasped. "Shoot me with it! Kill me—" I kept squeezing the trigger as she moaned and gasped, squeezing my neck so tightly she was beginning to choke me.

With the barrel of the gun between her legs, we lay on the bed as the sun beat against the glass.

Sad that she'd failed to draw blood with the pistol, she thrust her fingers into herself, hunting some blood but found none. "I wanted to bleed like the lamb—" she said. Falling back across the bed, her small ribs were going up and down with her breath, she put her fingers into her mouth and closed her eyes. I reached over and tucked my hand into her crotch. She was leaking sweet liquid. I brought my hand up and placed it on her mouth. Her tongue came out—licking. Her other hand slid down her stomach and busied itself in her crotch. Lapping at my hand and fingers, she began to moan, stretching her legs out straight.

Pictures were going around in my head and when I opened my eyes again the sun had disappeared from the skylight. The walls were again black, with no reflections. "Who did you call on the phone?" I asked.

"Oh, Robert," she said, "because I want to have my skates, so he can get them where we were in Pigalle. My backpack is there and he will find it. I had to run from being followed."

"That policeman again?" I asked.

She shook her head. "Somebody else. I worried about somebody snooping on me and that is how I came to be without my skates. I do not even have my socks! And I am tired—I am sleepy now but I feel good that I am staying with you. It made me afraid to be in Pigalle last night because I was being followed."

"That policeman?" I asked.

"I don't know. It was a bad feeling."

"If you've lost your skates," I said, "we'll get you another pair."

"Robert will find my backpack and my skates," she said, then seemed to remember something. "But my socks! I left them under a table. So they will be swept away by someone who is sweeping the floor and will be *gone*!"

"They're only socks," I said. "You have other socks—"

She shook her head. "I only have my backpack now. I have a toothbrush and these are my clothes that I wear in the video. Those were my socks..."

I sat down on the bed beside her. "Where do you *live*, Juju? You must have some place where you go to—"

She shrugged. "I do not live anywhere."

"But you stay somewhere—"

"I was sleeping at Robert's hotel and watching television, but now he has David from the desk sleeping with him. I stayed on the floor one night but David got mad." She looked at me. "I lived with Jean Paul, you see..." She smiled suddenly, nodding. "I think Robert is fixing it so I will have some place to stay, even if it is in Pigalle. That is where we went yesterday—to see this place where I will stay."

"I see," I said, reaching for the bottle of ouzo. I filled a glass and handed it to her. She swallowing most of it, making an uncomfortable face. "You should sip it," I said. "It'll knock you out."

She nodded again. "Good," she said. "I like to be knocked out. Then I do not have to wonder what I am going to do or how I will get my money from people." The heat was stoking the flat as we finished the ouzo on empty stomachs, lounging on the bed, Juju on one end in the black silk robe. She had the long black and yellow dotted scarf up behind her head but kept drawing it across her face as I talked about the Japanese script. Her head propped as it was, the roll of baby fat beneath her chin protruded and her cheeks looked wide across the face, the eyes seeming wider apart. For just an odd moment she didn't look like the same girl.

Finishing the ouzo, I swung my legs off the bed and reached for the unopened Merlot. "I'll let you have some money," I said. "You won't be able to get around without any money."

She smiled. "Oh, what a relief that will be," she said. "I will pay you back when the godfather gets my money to me..."

"We won't worry about that right now," I said. She was gazing at the corkscrew knife and opener as I twisted it into the cork. "Is that silver?" she asked. I said yes. She said, "Is the knife blade very sharp?"

"It's very sharp," I said.

"Monsieur Pinaud gave me a silver candlestick. It was old and had the face of an angel on it like the round moon face of the angel you can see in Montmartre Cemetery. He also drank the same Merlot wine and put it in crystal glasses. I can wet my finger and run it around the edge of the crystal and make it sing!"

"Who is Pinaud?" I asked.

"The undertaker who drank wine with Jean Paul. *That* wine," she said, pointing to the bottle. "It is how I met Jean Paul—through Pinaud who is also the art collector, but he has a mortuary where he has some of Jean Paul's paintings—the little pictures that are from a long time ago. They are in the magazines, too!"

"You knew Pinaud before you were staying with Jean Paul?" I asked.

"Yes. I went to the gallery with Pinaud to see Jean Paul's paintings. That is how I became a model for Jean Paul, and then we fell in love."

"Jean Paul gave you money?" I asked.

"Certainly! That is what I earned posing for the goddess," she said.

"What is that?" I asked.

"It is one of the white sculptures of the people in the boxes that Jean Paul made. Of course, I spent the money while I was with Jean Paul. My rollerblades—Jean Paul bought those for me.

I had an old pair that were not nearly as good. I gave the other pair away to the boy that is Tanyous' friend. He doesn't speak French very well. With the new rollerblades, it is such a feeling of freedom. I don't know if I can describe it to you—"

I drank the Merlot from the bottle and passed it to Juju.

"I had a ring that is gold that Jean Paul gave me. It belonged to his mother."

"He gave you a ring that belonged to his mother?"

"And he gave me an anklet of hers that is very old and made of solid gold."

"He was very generous to you," I said.

"Yes..." she sighed. "I will never forget Jean Paul. It's a shame that Pinaud has some of the little paintings. It is terrible because Jean Paul's work was very alive and now the ones that I believe to be the most alive are in the undertaking parlor."

"You must take me to see it, and to meet this Pinaud," I said.

"Oh, I cannot do *that*!" she said. "The man introduced me to Jean Paul, and that was Pinaud being generous to me. What happened was that Jean Paul fell in love with me when we saw one another. Pinaud was very jealous and said, 'I can never see *that* person again!' Of course, he meant me..."

"So you'd had a relationship with this undertaker?" I asked.

She shook her head, tipped the bottle and drank, then handed it back to me. "You can not say it was a 'relationship' because he had me in a coffin, you see. I lay in a coffin and he looked at me. He would not let me open my eyes." She smiled weakly, shrugging. "He would take pictures of me and I can imagine what else this man did while my eyes were closed."

"How did he make you keep your eyes closed?" I asked.

"He paid me to keep them closed at first, and then he would not give me the money if I opened my eyes. After a while he did not trust me to keep my eyes closed because he thought I was peeking, so he made me put on goggles that people wear under water. Only these goggles were painted black so I could not see through them. That was my 'relationship', as you call it, with one of Jean Paul's big shot patrons."

"Did he touch you while you were in the coffin?" I asked.

"He did not touch *me*," she said, "but he asked me to wear silver slippers. Oh, they are high-class dancing shoes, and I would wear these in the coffin and then I would leave them with him when I left. He told me the dancing shoes were made of real silver. I didn't care about him and I was only modeling so there would be some money. That was before Jean Paul fell in love with me. He saw the photographs of me in the coffin and said that I was beautiful, and asked Pinaud to bring me to the galley so he could meet me."

"Whatever happened to the silver candlestick?" I asked.

"Oh, that was at Jean Paul's," she said. "Then it was in my backpack but is gone now." She sighed. "My ring and my gold anklet are gone, too." She reached for the wine and said, "Everything is gone, Jake... It all goes because of the mistakes."

"What 'mistakes'?" I said. "You're young enough to get ten times all that back."

She was shaking her head. "No, I do not think I will live to do that. I think I will not live very long, but I do not want to die— not for real like Mark Lajos is now dead. I only want to be dead as one is in dreams—" She stared to cry and I grabbed her. I took her in my arms and held her, sort of rocking her. I didn't know what day it was or whether I was expected somewhere. We stayed that way for several moments and I could feel her breathing heavily. I looked at her. She was asleep.

I laid her back and covered her with the leopard-skin sheet. Stretching out beside her, I closed my eyes. My head became a tank of liquid for passing fish. Some moved slowly—others darting like sharks, teeth bared, colliding into bodies and fastening hungry jaws. Then the bigger electronic fish—giant blinking antennas on top of their heads. They moved the slowest, their broad, complicated tail fins wavering in the ink of my brain. I felt removed as if a tube were pushed in my head and sensations sucked out into some bag hanging from the mouth on a vacuum.

I reached to the floor for the bottle, gulped wine, then I tipped it to her mouth. She sucked in it, her lips around the neck and inching on the glass. She gagged, coughing the wine out of her mouth. Turning her head, her tongue reached for it on the mattress. I watched every detail—seeing myself as an unblinking eye that's not the artist anymore because my vision was without the skill to reproduce anything out-living my skin.

The phone was ringing and I let it ring. Her cheek was in the wine like blood coming out of her mouth.

I inserted the silver rings into Juju's nipples and her belly button, and the larger one through the lips of her vagina. We finished the bottle of wine while I washed her feet in the bathtub. I kissed her feet and held her toes in my mouth.

Dressing quickly, she got into the black chaps and I helped her with the buckle at the rear. "You'll have to wear one of my shirts so it hangs over your butt," I said. "All that shows is your panties."

Fine golden hair like fuzz shined in the small of her back and I touched her skin, caressing the moistness, running my fingers down further into her panties. She turned her head partly to the wall and said, "I am going to be all wet—"

I pushed my fingers into the crevice of her buttocks and turning my hand, stuck my middle finger into her rear end. Her eyes shut and her mouth opened. "I want to kiss you there," I said. "I want to stick my tongue into you."

She began to moan a little as I steered her to the bed, put her face down and quickly pulled the black panties down off her rump without unbuckling the chaps. I spread her legs as far as I could and sunk my tongue into her. She reached around, grasping the cheeks of her ass to spread herself wider.

I came in my clean pants and just lay on her, my face against her bare, cooling ass as I caught my breath. She was stroking my head, then took hold of the iron bar of the bed frame.

"Jake—" she whispered.

"What is it?"

She said, "I want you to put handcuffs on my wrists and fasten them to this bed."

"You do?"

"Yes," she said. "It will make me feel as if I can put my feet into the ground and branches will then grow out of my body."

I turned her over and stared at her open, malleable face, touched her cheek and traced the shape of her skull. She opened her mouth and again took my fingers between her lips, sucking on them. She held my wrist with one hand and shoving her left hand down into the chaps, she worked quickly with her fingers between her thighs. In a moment she was gasping again, and in that same moment my cock was arching up hard and throbbing.

I got up, reached behind her, unbuckled the belt and pulled the chaps off her legs. Grabbing her naked body under me, her legs kicked out and I got between them and quickly thrust into her. She cried out—almost a shriek as I drove into her and smothered her mouth with my own—her tongue and mine moving like frantic snakes in a blind exit.

She jammed her hands up against the head rail, shoving her arms through the bars and bending them slightly, pulling and forced at the rails. I twisted her hair, grabbed her upper arms, pinning them, thrusting them outward and held her under me while I rammed in and out of her. She was almost hysterical—sobbing, squealing as I felt myself jumping and throbbing against her muscles.

Passing Eston's door on the way out of the building, we paused to listen but heard nothing. I didn't knock.

Outside, Juju passed the horse meat shop cautiously, looking both ways. "I do not want to be followed today," she said. "I am getting fed up and angry! I will carry your gun and shoot somebody following me. That will stop them."

"Yes," I said. "It would certainly discourage them."

"The world is made up of crazy people!" she said.

I agreed. We got Chinese food at the Left Bank Chop Suey and carried it with us through the flea stalls and junk shops. I could feel her suspiciousness at moments, but then she'd laugh and seem free of the thoughts. But they stayed with me—sort of lingering like a peculiar aftertaste. I caught myself looking around while she'd snoop in the stalls.

I bought her a luxurious 1940's black silk slip, and a high-waisted dress with copper rivets down the sides. She found an old leopard skin covered suitcase, and cried, "Oh, Jake! This matches the bed sheet and this is a real leopard!" We bought the moth-eaten suitcase and into it she packed our purchases, including new chartreuse socks and a Japanese kerchief, a Rolling Stones tee-shirt, two pairs of handcuffs and a couple lengths of dog leash chain. She said, "The chain makes me very excited and I'm getting all wet between my legs—" She clutched my arm, kissing my shoulder. "I have to pee," she said.

Off the boulevard, we found a passage crowded with bushes into which she snuggled. I took her suitcase while she squatted down, baring her bottom. Staring up at my face, she began to pee. She said, "I am thinking about the chains going so tight around my stomach that I cannot breathe..." She put her one hand between her legs, urinating over her hand. I watched her. Looking into my eyes, she brought her hand up to her face, opened her mouth and began to lick at her fingers.

Out of the bushes and still hungry, we drifted into the little cafe on rue Dauphine, swabbed some bread in the Chinese container, ordered sausage, French fries and mushrooms. I ordered a bottle of the Hungarian wine, "just for the hell of it," I said. She said, "You must have a lot of money, Jake. You buy wine that is so expensive."

I shrugged. "Easy come, easy go, as they say. Perhaps I'll start tossing it about like confetti—"

"No!" she said. "You cannot do that because you are an important man and that would be something bad to do."

"I'm a hack," I said. "A kind of plumber of the cinema. I clean the crap out of other people's pipes. Actually since I'm now installing my own pipes, the work's become so much easier. I don't have to think as much and the money's better. You'd be surprised how easy it is."

"Easy for you, Jake, but not for somebody else," she said. "And no matter what you say, you are a wonderful writer and know so many stories for the movies. I only know one story and it isn't even French!"

The waiter opened the wine, didn't fill the glasses but left the bottle on the table. I said to Juju, "What is your story about?"

"Oh, it is not *my* story," she said. "It is very old—about a noble English man named Edward Mordake. It is a true story that was told to me."

"Never heard of him," I said, filling our glasses.

"This was in the 17th century," she said. "He was the heir to so much, and he was so very rich, but he never claimed his famous title. He committed suicide when he was twenty-three years old. He lived in seclusion and did not even see his own family, but he was a very great scholar—and an intelligent man, and he was also a musician."

"Why did he kill himself?" I asked, cutting the sausage.

She drank, wiped her mouth and picked up her fork. "He was so very handsome," she said, "his face was like a statue of the gods. But on the back of poor Edward's head was another face— a beautiful girl's face that was lovely as a dream but as awful as the *devil*." She reached for the wine and refilled her glass. "The face of the girl was a little face—a mask occupying this small outside part of the back of Edward's head. The face seemed to be very intelligent but was *bad*, you see. It would be seen to sneer while poor Edward was sad and crying, and the eyes of this face would follow a person. The mouth would say things without stopping."

"What was it saying?" I asked.

"No one could know," she said, "because no voice could be heard—except by Edward. Only the lips would be moving and never stop. Edward swore he was kept awake because he could hear the face saying hateful things—his devil-twin, he said— which did not sleep but spoke to him forever of things that are only in *hell*! That's what he said. So, poor Edward says, 'Oh, this wicked demon puts before me terrible temptations, and for some unknown reason the wickedness of my forefathers has made this fiend a twin to me! Oh, I must crush it out of life even if I will die myself!' "Juju stopped, smiled and shoved some sausage into her mouth. In a dramatic tone, she said, "In spite of his doctors being very careful to keep Edward away from the poison, he was able to swallow some and said in a letter that the demon face must be destroyed before he was buried, 'for fear it keeps up the dreadful whisperings in my grave!'" She sighed. "And he was buried in a place that is a waste land and with no stone or even a mark for his grave..."

I said, "The black ship to hell. Who told you that story?"

"I have known it a long time—since I was little. It was somebody who was nice to a relative, but he was not nice to me. But you see, since I was not in love with that person, it does not matter. For me, ahh, he had no feelings except to use me as a little girl and to get himself excited so he could fuck me and have it over with. But he was like a machine—a hard machine that did hurt me."

"Who was he?" I asked.

"He was nobody. He took pity on a relative and he was generous to me."

"He gave you money?"

"Yes. It is how I kept myself and the relative alive for a whole winter. This was three winters ago or more—"

"You're very young—" I said.

"I was three years younger then but it hasn't made a difference in my life."

"You have slept with men for money, then?"

"No. I have never been a prostitute. I sleep with somebody and they are generous to me. I would not fuck somebody that I did not feel comfortable with. You must know that about me. Don't you sense such a thing in me?"

"Yes, I can sense that about you. You use sex as a means of communication. You like to communicate."

"Sometimes I think I'll go to Marseille and hide and not see anyone anymore. I will be like Bridget Bardot and hide from people. In my case, from these people I do not want to be around anymore. But not *you!*" she said. "I want to be around you very much."

"I'm so much older than you—" I said.

"Oh, that is only the American way of thinking. I don't think like that. A person is a person and it doesn't matter how old or how young one is. So when you say about me, 'Oh, she is so young to go to Japan, she is such a young one,' then that is your American thinking—the American part of your brain that speaks. When you were fucking me you did not think, 'Oh, she is so young—' Did you? No. Because that was not the American of your brain. It was the inside part. It is like you say—the black ship to hell. You do not say, 'She is too young for me to put my thing inside of her.' But no, you put it inside of me and then it is all right with you, and you do not think I am too young, anymore than I am thinking, 'Oh he is too old to put his thing inside of me.'"

"My American brain is stupid," I said. "It has always been stupid. If I've seemed like a moronic American, I am sorry."

She blushed. "You are making fun of me!" she said.

"I'm not," I said. "And to prove it to you I'm going to have you come and visit me in Japan."

She beamed, then frowned. "But when will you go to Japan?" I said I wasn't sure. Maybe soon. I had to finish the script. She said, "Then I hope I will not die before you have me come to Japan."

"If you do," I said, "I won't let you go to some unmarked waste land like poor Edward."

"Will Mark Lajos have a big grave in Hungary?" she asked.

"I imagine he will," I said. "Like Camus said about American lawns—the bigger they are, the greater the guilt."

"An angel stands on Jean Paul's grave in Père-Lachaise," she said. "It is the same size as I am because I was the model. It was not supposed to be for a grave when Jean Paul used me. One hand is out like this—" Juju got up and struck a pose, standing lightly as if on the tip of diving board but looking towards the horizon, one arm lifted, the hand faintly reaching but with the palm down, the little finger rising slightly as though lighter than air. "The angel is supposed to be asking for somebody to have hope. But the angel is me," she said, sitting down again. "It was supposed to be in a box—one of the mummies in the box, but now they have big wings that go down the back of the legs and are up here by the shoulders."

"I'd like to see it," I said. "I've never been to Perè Lachaise or any other cemetery in Paris."

"Oh, you have missed many sights. Jean Paul visited graves all the time and the catacombs. So he could commune, he said, like you say 'communi*cate*', to talk to the spirit of somebody dead."

I didn't know what the mummy people were. She said she was one of them—along with Elvis Presley and Frank Sinatra.

We walked north from the cafe to the Quai de Conti, heading to the gallery to see Vermond's 'mummy people'. A legless man scooting over the sidewalk on padded stumps, stopped and greeted JuJu. "Hello!" she said to him. "He is in Tanyous' video!" she told me, and joked about something to the man. He laughed—there were no teeth in his mouth. I reached down a handful of francs as Juju started skipping, her bare feet dirty again, the leopard suitcase bouncing at her side. The handcuffs and chains clattered inside the case and I kept flashing on her hands reaching through the rails of the bed.

She paused at the iron pole overlooking the river, handed me the leopard case and threw some twigs down into the water. "When I die," she said, "I don't want to have anything standing on top of me. I want to be put in the river."

"I'm afraid your policeman friend would be pretty quick to fish your body out," I said.

"No!" she said, and laughed. "I am saying when I get *cre*mated like Pinaud does at the crematorium. Then it is my ashes that can be thrown into the water—" She darted away from the rail, spinning around and running along the Quai. I wasn't going to be able to keep up with her.

"Don't run away!" I called after her.

She turned around and jumped up into the air a little. She was very light—a lot of bounce to her. "I will not run away!" she said. "We are going to learn to speak Japanese, aren't we, Jake?"

We roamed Saint Germain in the bright sun and near the square, Juju stopped and looked around with a somewhat suspicious frown. I asked what was wrong and she said nothing. "Where is this gallery?" I asked.

"It is not far," she said. "Two more blocks."

By the time we reached the gallery on rue Gueneguad, her face was glistening with sweat. We stepped into the shade of a doorway while she wiped her cheeks and her breasts with her new Japanese kerchief. She said, "Jake, wipe me down here..." and pulled up the front of the shirt and stuck her thumb into the waist of the chaps. I reached the cloth down the front of the chaps curved it into her crotch, feeling the ring in her cunt. When I brought it out, she said, "How does it smell, Jake?"

Her eyes were shining as I brought the cloth handkerchief to my face, covered my nose and mouth, staring at her. She stood on her naked tiptoes, pulled the handkerchief from my face and kissed me, reaching her tongue into my mouth.

She said, "I want you to fuck me right now..."

"I can't. We're in a public doorway..." I kissed her again, feeling her breasts with the rings in her nipples. "I want to put the chain in the rings," I said.

A moment later we walked into the white-washed gallery and she said, "That is me! *Me!* This is what I wanted to show you—"

I stood in the center of the gallery surrounded by a half-dozen plaster-white, life-sized mummy figures half-embedded in boxes or crates.

Juju'd dashed straight ahead to one at the crown of the half-circle of mummies, an upper torso from hips to full head, the form at a half-turning angle, face averted three-quarters. The white plaster gave off a muted, almost iridescent glow. The form was embedded in white plaster half-sunk and encased in a white-painted crate less than a foot deep.

He'd cast Juju, all right, filled the mold with some epoxy or some substance, then cast the figure from the mold, which he apparently then sunk into another substance that appeared like a pool almost all white plaster of Paris.

"I am a goddess!" Juju said excitedly, standing next to the piece and striking an identical pose. The only difference I could see from Juju that he'd made with the piece called *Déesse*, was the hair. *Déesse* had long hair down to the waist that lay tangled atop of the pool closely surrounding her. He'd no doubt cast one or more lengthy wigs, sinking them into the plaster.

"It's wonderful," I said.

"I had to lay still for a *long* time with plaster all over me and on my face, but first he covered me with a thin plastic wrap like you put on cantaloupe."

That's where the lines came from—the wrinkles suggesting mummy wrapping, etched angularly and crookedly over the face and upper bodies of the pieces.

"You know I helped Jean Paul," she was saying, "because I used fine sandpaper and steel wool to smooth down the box he put my statue in." She went up on her toes again, this time kissing the face of the sculpture.

"Please do not touch the work!" the proprietor warned, crossing to Juju. She was a thin, rakish woman with a narrow chin and protruding, almost sharp cheekbones.

"But this *me*!" Juju said to her.

"Please do not touch the works..." the woman said again, her eyes dropping the length of Juju's leather-clad legs to her bare feet. Juju pouted as I moved past the figures in boxes of Elvis Presley and Frank Sinatra—odd, strange replicas turned into white mummies half sunk in white packing crates. Opposite these figures were three more—life-sized males in boxes—each one a hanged man. The coarse, plaster-coated hemp ropes were around each neck. One of the two figures looked familiar for some reason—a worn, haggard face. The middle figure, like a Christ centered between the other two, was a self-portrait sculpture of Vermond—hanged with the rope still around his neck.

I turned to look at Juju but she'd walked off and was leaning from the waist peering out the gallery doorway. She seemed very irritated, the annoyance of the proprietor having nothing to do with it. I followed her eyes across the street to a figure lurking in the shadow of a gate; almost part of the shade and gaunt, the dark overcoat seemed smeared against the darker wall. People moving back and forth but the figure was still as a garbage can.

I couldn't see eyes due to the large sunglasses but the mouth was like a slit, an almost lipless cut between the chin and nose. Something under one arm—a board or piece of black wood.

Juju'd cried out into the street. "You go away!"

"Please!" The woman, hushing her. "Please don't make disturbance. This is an *art* gallery!"

"But I do not want that person following me—" Juju said.

I remembered Claude mentioning a tall, ratty figure in an old coat. By the time I glanced back, whoever it was had been set into motion by Juju's yell and was heading south on rue Gueneguade. The motions were quick, the upper body stiff and barely moving, only the legs—going rapidly back and forth. "Who was that?" I asked.

"It is a mister nobody!" Juju said. "Like you have a Mister Potato Head in United States, and that is *no*body!"

"Please—" the woman started, but I smiled, nodding, and held up my hand.

"It's all right," I said. "The girl is an actress and I'd like discuss purchasing that goddess piece—*Déesse.* We can talk about it when the show is down..."

The woman beamed, and Juju said, "You would buy the one that is me? Really?"

Her moods vacillated between being pleased that I'd consider purchasing the sculpture, she thought I'd probably be buying it for her, and a kind of agitated state that kept her glancing around. She wouldn't tell me who might've been following her—"just nobody," she'd say.

She was hungry again, wanted something sweet and strong coffee– "Arabian coffee," she said, and we stopped at a cafe on rue de Seine. I had a glass of wine and asked about the hanged figures. Had Vermond talked about them? She said, "You see, Jean Paul had premonitions that he would kill himself. He would say, 'Juju, I might die by my own hand, you know.'"

"And what was your response to that?" I asked.

"Oh, I could say nothing to Jean Paul. He lived in a tiny pocket of the universe where so very few people live, and told me his loneliness might drive him to be insane. That was what he told me, and said that at such a time he might be responsible for causing his own death."

Stuffing down a pastry, she went on, "He talked about people that were tortured by the Catholics, and he did not like the Catholics. He told me how they were tortured–such as their skin being pulled off of their bodies, and he talked about the ones that were hanged. When I met him through that man Pinaud, Jean Paul was working on the first man in the box that was hanged. The model was a young actor–I don't remember his name... Jean Paul was coating him in the grease, the lard that he put on me later so the plaster would not stick to the skin."

She asked for another pastry and dunked it into her coffee while I asked for a second glass of wine, thinking I should have ordered a bottle. "The actor," Juju said, "was going like this to me–" she motioned blowing kisses, "and Jean Paul was very upset. His face got *very* red and his forehead was all covered with lines. He kicked the actor out of the studio and did not have any more young men come to work for him. That's why the second hanged man is old. It was the man you gave money to who didn't have any legs. It did not matter that he did not have any legs because the boxes only go to the bottom of a person's body. The one of Jean Paul is of course Jean Paul, and he did that to himself–using the lard and the cellophane paper. But he had another artist–a very nice man, come and help him with the plaster because it is so heavy–"

She was rubbing her foot up and down on my skin, feeling under my pants leg. Licking the sugar and crumbs off her mouth, she slid down a little in the chair and I felt her foot suddenly reaching between my legs.

"Ohhh," she said. "You are thinking about me, aren't you, Jake?"

"Yes..." I said, putting my left hand on her bare foot.

"You like my feet," she said. "You kissed my toes in the bathtub. Now I am walking on the streets and they are dirty feet, and you are getting big in your pants. Do you like my dirty feet?"

"Yes," I said, swallowing wine, holding tightly to her foot as she pressed against my crotch.

"I would like you to kiss my toes now," she said, her heel working at my balls. "I would like you to lick them all over. You should kiss my toes and put them in your mouth. Stick your tongue between my toes like you did in the bathroom—"

"Stop it," I said. "I'm going to come if you keep pushing on me—"

"No!" she said, sitting up abruptly. "We will go to the exhibit! It is here now. I will take you to the place where Jean Paul took me, where he showed me how the people were tortured. Now it is back and you and *I* can go to it!"

We circled back on rue Guenegaud, again I was following Juju. I hurried after her, breathless at moments, hoping she wouldn't short-cut into some alley where I'd stumble into garbage and cats or cans or the homeless huddling against walls. I suspected her of threading some confusing trail in case she was still being followed. I didn't say anything.

We turned onto the very narrow, curving impasse, the walls of the buildings so close it appeared I could spread my arms and touch the fingers of both hands to the cool stone structures. The walls bowed and leaned slightly for a half a block, then opened to a wider street, rue de Nevers, over which hung a large black banner *LES INSTRUMENTS DE TORTURE ET DE MORT.*

Juju spun around in the middle of the street. "See? This is where we are going!"

"Okay," I said. "Let's take a look."

The exhibit took up the a partitioned area of the first floor in a lime-white warehouse, and a smaller cellar beneath the street's surface.

She raced about the displays excitedly as if babbling through a tour. The guillotine, the Virgin of Nuremburg—a spike-filled metal chamber. She pointed at the chastity belts. "To control women," she said. "And these are leg irons, Jake. And for a woman who is accused of slander, you see this is a metal mask with a mouth gag that makes her unable to speak!"

"Fascinating," I said. She showed me a "crusher," to break the leg and arm bones, and hurried me to the hanging cage.

"In this cage," she said, "one is left to starve to death, so they turn into a skeleton and the bones fall apart!" She struck a pose in front of the cage. A sign said the device was last used in Sicily in 1928. Juju said, "You can keep me forever in this cage."

"You would die," I said.

"You would have my skeleton! Just like the Japanese man you are writing about. You could clean off the meat and have my bones polished clean."

I asked when Vermond had brought her to the exhibit and she said, "Oh, Jean Paul came here when it was open last year. He drew pictures. I climbed into the cage and he drew my picture. He had to help me up into it. It is big, I told him, he would fit into it if I had not been occupying it. So he lifted me down—"

Juju suddenly put her arms around my neck and kissed me. "We must go downstairs," she said, "so you can hear the screaming of the woman being tortured and killed!" Oddly, we were the only visitors in the gallery.

The narrow, brightly lit stairway wound down almost at a spiral, and opened at the bottom level into a small room—more an alcove, with a skeleton hanging on the wall beside a locked cage.

There was a long wooden table—a victim was hanged on the

rack-like end of it, the rope fixed around the neck while the ankles and feet were clasped under a kind of yoke that could be drawn lower on sliding extensions, thus causing slow strangulation. Upon the table sat a reel to reel recorder, and Juju pushed the play button. We stood there listening to a series of screams—supposedly those of some woman being tortured. "She dies at the end," Juju said. "She keeps screaming and screaming and then she chokes to death and dies—"

She pulled open the top and put her fingers into the rings in her nipples. "Jake—" she said. "Put the chain in here—the chain we bought—put it in the rings."

Opening the leopard skin case, she whipped out the chains and handcuffs, and I took the chain and carefully threaded it through the nipple rings. She quickly unclasped the chaps and pulled them down in front, hurriedly guiding the chain through the ring in her navel, then reaching down to her crotch. "Here—put the chain through the ring down here."

"What if someone comes down here—" I started to say.

"They will turn around and go back up the steps, Jake. Anyway we can hear them coming down the stairs—"

"Not with the screaming going on—"

"You are deaf, Jake—I can hear somebody if they are coming!" She had the chain through the ring in her stomach and now looped through the ring on her cunt. She scooted up onto the dark oak torture table, fastening the handcuffs to one wrist. "Put it on my other hand—" she said.

I started to and she said, "No! Do it behind my back—handcuff me behind my back so it is like it is real, Jake. Do it tight!" I fastened the cuffs on her wrist, her arms behind her back and laid her down on the table. She said, "Is it in my cunt ring, Jake?"

"Almost," I said. I slipped the chain through the ring—the length of links running across her breasts, down through her navel and into the ring between her legs. I had both ends of the chain in my hands.

"Pull on it—" she said. "Pull it on it gently at first so I can feel how tight it is."

I pulled on the ends of the chain, looking at her ass between her legs, then pushed her legs up. Pulling the chaps lower and still holding the chain in one hand, I unbuckled the waist belt that held the two legs together and jerked the panties upwards. A wetness was leaking out of her and I ran my fingers into it and down back between her legs into her ass. I pulled out my cock and pushed it against her ass with her legs held up.

"Yes—yes!" she said. "Pull on the chain- pull until you see it stretching my tits and my cunt—!"

My cock went all the way into her ass and I pulled on the chain ends, taking it doubled in my fist. It seemed to yank her breasts downwards while pulling her vagina lips upwards as if to fold her in half at the middle.

I was afraid if I pulled harder the chain would jerk the rings out of her nipples—tearing the flesh or ripping the lips below. Her nipples were stretching into long points and she kept moaning and telling me to pull harder. Thrashing her head back and forth while I fucked her in the ass, her cries were a chorus to the screams on the tape, and I felt myself exploding up into her as if my cock shot forward like a flame from a gun.

But the brand was in my brain. The picture of the dead artist having done the same thing with her on the same table in the same dungeon.

She said no.

I didn't ask her point blank, but played around with the words. She'd never worn the handcuffs. The rest of it? She didn't know. She couldn't remember. It wasn't important.

Leaving the torture exhibit, I thought I spied the over-coated figure lurking in the Impasse, and I said, "Is that the potato head again?"

"Oh, no," she said. "It makes no sense." She tapped her head. "A crazy person. If we ride in a taxi nobody can follow us."

Was that Wednesday or Thursday? Monday I'd called LeeFeldt

in New York. I was going to Marseille for a couple days—recuperating from the vampire movie and Mark's "tragic end" that was filling the tabloids and television.

What had happened to Tuesday, I wondered. It didn't seem to matter.

Juju'd been in there earlier—or had that been the day before? I was waking up in the middle of the day and she was gone. My head was revolving like a lighthouse beam searching through fog.

All I could think of was the way she'd been sitting in the chair. The sun laying in through the skylight, casting a long shadow to the right like an elongated caricature of the flapper days, smoking and painting her toenails. *Fado* music was pouring out of the portable deck she'd dragged in. Wearing only the black kimono with the yellow dragon, she'd bring her foot up onto the chair and the silk would slide, showing the shadow at her crotch. She'd brush at hair or chase strays from her forehead and I'd wondered what she'd be like in the States, sitting in a chair the same way with the sun on her. She reminded me of the sea for some strange reason, water sliding across wet sand, slipping back and sucking into the deep.

The grotesque idea came to me that I would not be able to let her loose. I'd pack her up and take her to Japan. She'd have to stay—but how? It was bizarre and ridiculous. But right at that moment—with those thoughts as she'd sat with the sun lapping at her calves and the fine down glistening like tiny follicles of gold, the same with the center of her chest between those girlish breasts, a sinking plane, pitching down her belly and touched with the same glittering blonde—some sharp sound had sprung from the street and she'd brought her face up—averting slightly—a motorcycle? Her ears perked like an animal's. Sensing safeness, her eyes dropped again to her toenails and the tiny brush in one hand, her other fingers holding one toe away from the other. She'd looked up and smiled, eyes shadowed, the lids silken, a darkness without depth; two holes in her face that peeped into some place beyond me. It came in a passing thought that nothing good was going to come the girl's way. I could sense with a kind of rapidness of heart and a quivering inside—deeper than my stomach, somewhere in the spine.

We'd gone to the Red Egg. I remembered music—loud, almost crashing. The room seemed to be spinning in motion, packed with moving bodies and rainbows of lights. They'd been filming her dancing on rollerblades, lights rigged over the jammed floor and Juju centered—tight black leotards, that sleeveless military shirt opened down the front and her breasts swinging free, bared, the rings I'd chained that morning or the day before aglow in the strobe of white light—blue and red light—green flashing, then back to the blinding white.

Al was the tall one with the video camera, a long tail of black hair woven together at the back of his head and reaching between his shoulder blades. The other one, Tanyous, right at my side—his face an inch from mine to be heard over the din of music. I couldn't hear him. Something about the black ship to hell I'd told Juju about. No—I said I hadn't told her about the black ship, I yelled. She'd told me about the guy with the girl's face on the back of his head.

Tanyous couldn't hear me. He pretended to—nodding, talking. Something about getting money from a video distributor.

"I hate Disneyland on the skirts of Paris!" he said.

"So do I!" I told him, yelling back.

"We should burn it down!" he said.

"No good—" I started to say. We couldn't talk. It's what their video was about, he'd said. "The collapse! The phoenix is Juju—" he was saying. He was working—he kept bringing me drinks. He had a bunch of papers and pencils tucked in the pockets of his red vest, another pocket full of money.

Juju had the shirt off and was whirling on the crowded floor in a tight, spinning circle. Bodies lined the walls. The air was smoke and sweat and I had trouble keeping my eyes on her because the mass was moving around like a giant, tipping, merry-go-round circling the band into the center where Juju was spinning. You were either swept along in the Mecca-like rotation or jettisoned on your own.

Then I was outside—I remembered the sack in my pocket and I had trouble getting it out and the bottle to my mouth. French music—I was in another bar. I couldn't remember leaving the Red Egg or where I wound up.

Now I was on the bed. I felt sunburned.

She was on the bed with me. She was chained. I turned my head and looked at her. She was gagged. Her eyes were open and she was looking at me. She shook her legs, rattling the chain looped through the frame of the bed. The mattress squished beneath her, wet from her piss, our sweat and the hot water I'd poured over her body.

It was coming back now.

Pressing the fingers of my left hand to her chest, I felt her rapid heart and could see her throat turning red. I untied the gag from her mouth and when I squeezed her nipples her eyelids dropped and her nostrils flared like a colt's. She said, "I can't stop coming when I do—"

Her hands were swollen from the steel and I was about to unlock the handcuffs. "No—not yet," she said. She closed her eyes, breathing deeply. I bent over her, touching the skin of her stomach. "I want to taste it again," she said.

My cock was on fire—red, bruised almost, but I crawled up, taking it in my hand and stuffing it into her mouth. Her hands opened and closed, clenched in the handcuffs. She began sucking frantically—breathing in air around me because she couldn't get enough through her nose. Coming again, she seemed to shake and jerk like an epileptic. I throbbed into her throat until I couldn't take the touch of her tongue and slid out like a dog. I curled down against her in the warm heat.

Sun was coming in through the skylight.

The chain clanked when she suddenly kicked and I scrambled up to unlock the handcuffs around her ankles. I pulled the links through the iron posts and let them clatter to the floor. I unlocked the handcuffs at her wrists. She lay there, her eyes closed. For a second the thought skipped through my head that I'd die.

I said, "We have to eat."

"Oh, yes," she said, sitting up.

"We'll go to a very elegant cafe," I said.

"Is the water still in the bathtub?" she asked.

"I think it is," I said. "I didn't pull the chain."

"I will go sit in the tub and wash." She got up. "Did you black out again?"

"Was it night when I handcuffed you?" I asked.

"It was this morning. There was no light, Jake."

"I don't remember the night," I said. "When were you skating at the Red Egg?"

"We got my skates from Robert at the hotel the day before yesterday. Then we went to hear Tanyous. Al was shooting the film—"

"Yes," I said.

"You drank and were very funny, Jake. We danced. You swung me around and around." I couldn't remember but I nodded. "Then we fucked all night," she said. "We drank saki yesterday and you told me the Japanese story about the man eating the girl's flesh."

"Yes..." I said. "Okay. I remember."

"We drank more saki last night," she said. "We tried to go see Eston but he was not there. Che Che said he was at the dog fight with the hunchback and the African lady."

She went into the bathroom and turned on the water. "It is cold!" she called out. "I will run some water that is hot into it." I listened to her splashing around in the tub and then she said, "When you write about this girl in the Japanese story, do you think she feels pain when she is murdered?"

"I haven't thought about that part of it," I said.

"Does the Japanese man think about her pain while he is killing her?" she asked.

"He thinks only that by killing her will he possess her completely," I said. "Maybe not the act of *owning* her, but having reached some depth in the condition he's after."

I heard her getting up—her wet feet on the floor. "What is the condition?" she asked.

"I suppose something in the human condition," I said.

"So that is what you write about," she said, the towel around her, coming out of the bathroom. "But tell me what he thinks in his mind," she said, walking to the chair, the water dripping from her legs and back. "What he will do to her—will he kill her quickly—like sticking a knife into her heart?"

"No," I said. "He kills her slowly, not painfully, but slowly so he knows everything she feels and that way allowing *him* to feel. He doesn't feel anything, you see."

She sat down in the chair. "But he is a killer—"

"He sees that as his passion—obliquely, you understand. *She* is his passion. He hasn't killed anyone before—"

"And afterwards? What does he do?"

"Well, the story is only about her murder and what he does to her. But in the act, he does come to feel a recognition. He sees what the serial killer is made of. He seeks the situation again, you see. Only it can't happen a second time because he has already killed her."

"But he can kill some other girl—" she said.

"Well, he doesn't. I've told you this story only concerns his obsession about the girl and her murder."

"So you don't know if he does go out to kill some other girl?"

"Juju—" I said, "it's a *screen*play I'm writing. I'm making up most of it right out my head. The character vanishes when I finish writing the damn thing."

"And in the story," she asked, "he puts parts of her body in the refrigerator?"

"Yes. He gradually eats sections of her. That's the main Japanese input into the movie, the real case this is based on. That's what happened."

"What parts of her does he eat?" she asked.

"Most of her body except the stomach, the spleen, intestines and other insides and maybe the lungs. I'm not sure. I don't think he does anything with her lungs. These he gets rid of in the river in a weighted plastic bag. But the rest he cooks and seasons and devours—the liver, the kidneys, her brain and her heart."

"He eats her brain, Jake?" she asked, her eyes wide.

"Yes."

"Does he throw her bones in the river also?"

"No. He actually plans to have the bones put together so he can hang the skeleton intact."

"Hang?" she said.

"Suspended—like you see a medical specimen. Have it all together. He makes an arrangement for her bones to be prepared like this, and it's basically the blackmailing of this medical technician into doing it. Both of them boil the skeleton and wire it together. That's how the killer gets caught. His need to have the skeleton and forcing the other to go along with him."

"He falls in love with her skeleton," Juju said. "He has a love affair with the girl's bones."

"In a manner of speaking. Once he's done the deed he can go no further than obsessing over the bones. They are perfect and lovely and white and no doubt just like your bones."

"Would you put my bones together and suspend them?" she asked.

"If you'd like," I said. "Are you planning on shedding your skin soon?" She nodded. "That's absurd," I said.

"No, it is not absurd," she said. "Perhaps I am planning my own death right now. But I would not want to feel pain—not the pain of a violent death."

I said, "I don't believe you're planning such a thing. How would you do it?"

"Cause it to happen," she said. "Like you put parts of this story together to make it happen, so I can be putting pieces together. I know I can do this. Like the Japanese man who has made his own accomplishment."

"It's power," I said. "He commits the ultimate act with this girl and while he's impelled to repeat it—with *her,* or at least into gaining the same satisfaction, he can't because he's killed her once. He comes to learn that his own sense of overpowering curiosity has carried him beyond reason."

"So he goes crazy?" she asked.

"Well, he's fairly crazy as the story progresses to carry him to the extremes with the girl."

"Would you do that to me?" she asked. "Kill me and eat me?"

I just stared at her. "No..." I said.

"Does eating me not seem appealing to you?" She let the towel drop open and put her hands on her breasts.

"Are you talking about an oral—sexual situation or are you talking about the removal of organs?"

She was pursing and puckering her lips deliciously. "I'm talking about the removal of organs..." She began to lick her lips. "I want to eat my own tits," she said, massaging her breasts. Sinking back into the pillows, she cupped her breasts from beneath, pressing them upwards on her small rib cage. She took the nipples between her fingers and pulled outward, stretching them.

"Doesn't that hurt?" I asked.

"No—it makes heat in me. I can come when I do this... You want to see how I can come when I do this?

"Yes," I said. Her face lowered, her eyes going from nipple to nipple—the right—then the left, and then back again. She took her right nipple in both fingers of both hands and tugged it outward, elongating it twice its length, more than they'd stretched in the dungeon.

"Doesn't that hurt?" I asked again.

She nodded quickly, and then her eyes closed and she squeezed at her breasts, pinching the nipples quickly—mouth dropping open a little and her head rolling slowly from side to side with her rapid intake of breath. "But I like it—I want to be hurt. I want pain—" Her stomach began to tremor and she sucked it in, breathing fast and hard for a moment. She groaned softly then almost whimpered. Her hands went limp. I could see the faint sheen of sweat coming over her skin and face. She sighed.

"You came"? I asked.

"Oh, yes—" she said, nodding. "Small... It was not a big come for me." She opened her eyes, heavy lidded, sleepy-looking. She smiled, showing those even small, teeth. She nodded again, pulling closed the silk robe over her reddened breasts.

"Are you going to be my lover until I die, Jake?"

"You aren't dying," I said, "and I'm old enough to be your father and a half."

"No! You are not serious—"

"Well, practically serious."

"That is not true. You are imagining that you are old or that I am so young like a little girl."

I said, "I'll be fifty in July…"

"You're a Cancer," she said. "Somebody with so many secrets. You are attracted to secrets…or you keep secrets. And you play games with people. You play with some people like toys because you are attracted to them but you can not stay with them… That is what I was told about Cancer people."

"That's very observant of you," I said. "But what I am going to do with you?"

"I can accompany you to Japan!" she said. "I will be your geisha girl." I didn't say anything and she said, "So perhaps you will not stay with me—but I am Cancer, too. You are one of the people of the moon."

"And you're my moon girl," I said.

She nodded. "I am the moon girl."

"You shine in the dark," I said, staring at her legs drifting open and closed. "I want to kiss you right now down there," I said. "Your sweet place where I've put my 'thing' into you. I want to taste you, Juju."

"I want you to," she said, sinking back again. She stared at me intently as I pushed the robe away and ran my hands over the glass smooth thighs, feeling the faint fuzzy blonde, touching the mound of hair—a kind of thin shape like a short tornado disappearing into the pink folds between her legs. I bent and kissed her thighs and short soft hair. My tongue slid down between her legs as she spread her thighs and raised herself upwards on the edge of the seat.

Knees on the floor, I pressed my mouth to her, hungrily licking, sticking my tongue into her and forcing it to squirm in her. Coming again, she clutched at my hair, my head, pressing my face into her until I felt my upper teeth cutting into my lip.

"Bite me!" she said. "*Bite* me!"

I grabbed myself and pulled hard and fast while I opened my mouth around her cunt and let my teeth press into her as I sucked the juices from her body until I felt my insides self-straining. Though I didn't want to move, I had to roll my face away from her to breathe.

Moments later I got up and slumped on the bed, my head falling back. She was looking down at herself and ran her hands down her stomach. She said, "You did not leave any teeth marks on my skin..." Her fingers slid into herself, massaging or feeling back and forth as if exploring its shape and depth. "That was nice, Jake, my dear. You made me come right away. Now you did not think I am too young to do that to me with your mouth, did you?"

"No," I said.

"Would you do that to me if I was only fourteen years old? What if I told you I am not seventeen but I am only fourteen years old?"

Raising my head, I looked at her. Her eyes were sparkling slightly and she had a funny little smile. "Are you only fourteen?" I asked. "If you are, I think we'd best reconsider my American brain."

"But if I am just as I am now?" she said. "If I am no different than I am now? Would you have said you could not eat me because I am only fourteen years old?"

I shook my head weakly. "You keep asking these perplexing— somewhat unnerving questions—unnerving in their unpredictability."

"I am sorry if I make you uncomfortable," she said.

"It would make me considerably more uncomfortable if you *are* telling the truth because it's a legal matter." I said, "Even in Paris. We aren't in Japan or Tangier. You should tell me if you're fourteen years old."

"What would you do if I did tell you that?" she asked.

"I'm afraid I'd have to discontinue this relationship for the time being," I said. "For a few more years, at least."

She laughed. "Well," she said, "certainly I am not fourteen

years old. I am almost eighteen years old, in fact."

"When will you be eighteen?"

"This June," she said. "The end of it. I am a Gemini—but I am a Cancer, too, because I am in the middle."

"You're just turning eighteen," I said.

"Yes. Does your American brain say that I am not old enough to be the girl of your dreams?"

"No," I said. "It doesn't say that. It says I don't have a girl of my dreams."

She was fingering herself and I was watching her. "Then I am the girl of dreams..." she said, pulling open the robe again, the slick, silk material slithering against her skin. Her stomach tightened as her hands met on the insides of her thighs. She pulled apart the lips of her vagina—her belly moving slightly, sort of rolling, and her clitoris and fine muscles protruded slightly as the yellow stream trickled from her. "I am peeing," she said.

I didn't move. She reached out, seized my hand and brought it beneath her crotch. Another stream, stronger, covered my hand with its wet heat. She dropped her head back and began to come again. The muscles in her neck stuck out like thin cords and her skin turned flushed pink. I cupped my hand against her as she pee'd and her whole body shook for a moment. She gasped and slumped almost lifeless.

As I stared at her breasts, my cock came up straight again. Her mouth was open, half-panting, and she crawled out of the chair and between my legs. Arms about my thighs, she took my cock into her mouth. A few deep strokes, swallowing me into her throat past the back of her mouth, and I was coming. She fastened her mouth on me, sinking and sliding so deep her jaws pushed at my pubic bone. I came into her throat and had to push her head away.

Quiet for a few minutes, then she giggled a little. Getting to her feet, she hurried to the bathroom while I lay back on the bed, my feet on the floor. I could still feel her in my toes and in the ends of my fingers.

If she was fourteen years old I'd be arrested. Maybe that's why the inspector-character cop was tagging around. Worse, with scapegoat Mark in the ground, my ex-wife could file criminal charges against me *in absentia*...

Light in the flat went gray, then brighter, then darker again as the sky changed colors through the gritty, overhead glass. Blue greens and a yellow the color of sap. I imagined a face in the age-blotched glass: a cat—a jaguar, front claws hooked to the metal ridge of the skylight enough for its neck to stretch and those yellow eyes staring down at me.

Quickly, with a jerking spasm, I sat up and grabbed another bottle of wine and the corkscrew. She was doing something in the bathroom—the water running, I could hear her as I opened the knife blade, cut the metal from the top of the bottle and twisted the screw into the cork. Popping it out, I set the corkscrew on the credenza and tipped the bottle to my lips. Looking up, there wasn't any jaguar, nor the sound of claws or nails on the metal or the glass. The big cat was in my head.

"Are you coming back?" I called out. She said yes. The toilet flushed. It made a gurgling, rattling noise.

Juju floated back into the room, her face covered with some sort of white salve. Not just salve—though zinc-white in color like a clown in a pantomime, but also a white powder sprinkled down her breasts and stomach. The stark wedge of white skin glared out against the black robe. She was carrying a towel carefully folded and came with quick, mincing little steps.

"What are you doing?" I asked.

"I am your geisha girl," she said, stopped and bowed with the towel extended in both hands. Squatting down, she started wiping the edge of the chair and the floor.

Staring at her as I took another drink, I said, "Japanese geishas get fucked a lot. Would you like to get fucked a lot?"

"Yes," she said. "I would like to get fucked. It makes me feel complete. I am whole when I am getting fucked. The harder I get fucked the more it makes me feel that I am all together."

"Do I fuck you hard enough?" I asked.

"No..." she said. "But that is not because of you, Jake, my dear.

Because I remember how hard I can get fucked and nobody fucks me that hard. Only once—but I told you. He wasn't nice. But he fucked me hard…"

She stopped her cleaning to place the towel against her face. "I smell my pee…" she said, her eyes closing. She inhaled deeply, bunching the towel about her face. Then she seemed to have trouble breathing. Sudden gasps. I thought something was wrong. She sucked in her breath, trembling. Her face came around to me and she kind of fell against my legs, eyes wide and excited, her hands feeling my bare skin, reaching for my cock and balls. She kissed and licked my thighs, running her hand up my chest.

Grabbing my hand and squeezing it, she bent my fingers inward to my palm like a claw and scraped it across her chest. Her nipples jerked. She shocked me, slapping herself across the face. "Hit me!" she said. "Slap me!"

I swiped my hand across her face as she slapped at her own breasts and bare thighs. "Now choke me!" she said. I grabbed her neck and began squeezing. It felt so small in my hands. "*Use* something to choke me!" She tore off the robe and wrapped one sleeve around her neck. Squatting naked now, she yanked and pulled at it with both hands. I took the silk in my grip and applied pressure as she gasped for air. She couldn't speak. Her eyes were wide. It was fascinating. Frantic—not fear, but a frantic look that was so intense it scared me. She was like something wild I was trying to get a grip on—trying to capture.

Climbing up on her knees, she then reached across my arm to the credenza and seized the corkscrew—the blade was open. Taking it with the cork in her palm, she held the knife point between two fingers and instantly ran it across her skin on her lower ribs between her stomach and breasts. A find red line trailed the blade and quickly teardrops of blood trickled towards her crotch.

"Oh, look!" she said. "Look what I'm doing—it's blood!" Again she streaked the blade on her body, this time from the other side, another angle—a wider cut across her chest. Blood came out of it instantly.

"Oh!" she cried out, running her other hand over her stomach and breasts, smearing blood on her cheeks and forehead, licking at her hand, lapping at the blood on her fingers. The sleeve dropping from her neck, she pressed her blood-smeared hand to my face. "Kiss it!" she said. "Taste it! Lick it—"

I got down on the floor with her—grabbed her hand and sucked on the bloodied fingers as she slashed the blade again across her stomach—this time deeper. The blood ran quickly, and the front of her torso was smeared with it She smudged it over her belly and her thighs and onto my face, gasping almost uncontrollably.

"Lick it—it's good! It's good!" she squealed as I pressed my face to her breasts and stomach, running my mouth back and forth, sucking at the blood leaking out of the red lines across her body.

"I'm cutting! I'm cutting!" she cried, thrusting the blade into my hands. "I can't stop coming! You do it! Do it—cut me!"

She scooted her bare ass back on the floor, drawing her legs up and apart, throwing her arms to the sides. She grabbed my hand and pulled me against her, twisting my wrist to push the knife point into her cunt. "Stick it in me! Stick it in me!" she cried. "Make blood come—You do it! Murder me!" She dug the tip of the blade into the flesh at the meeting of her upper thigh just on the edge of her lips.

Crying out in pain and gasping in orgasm—she pushed the tip of the blade into herself. She cried out again and I quickly pulled it out. Blood followed fast—dripping dark drops which she took into her hands and licked and pushed my face down to her crotch.

The blood was leaking into my mouth. I pressed my tongue to the slit she'd made and sucked in her blood. She dropped the knife and clutched my head—crying out all the while. Her silk robe tightened around my neck and she began pulling at it until I felt myself strangling.

I'd slept little for days but felt crisp, with a crackle to my step. The sun was gliding in and out of an overcast sky. I hadn't brought my rain coat. An old photo was in my mind of a man on a dog sled heading into a depthless land. My eyes took a sharp focus.

The squat detective was sitting at a cafe on Belles Feuilles, a block from Leefeldt's office. The smile on his thick lips was like something sketched on a hairy sack. Across the table from Marlet was another man, with a long gray face as though he suffered some heart or lung ailment.

"Monsieur Morgan!" the detective called, widening his eyes in mock surprise. He reached out his hand and I shook it. For an instant the image of handcuffs snapped in my thoughts. "We were just talking about the motion picture," he said, and introduced the gray man whose face had no expression. I couldn't see the eyes behind the narrow sunglasses. His hand felt cold and limp. Something about him being a forensic specialist. "Monsieur Morgan wrote the script for *Sucant du Sang*," Marlet said. "It should prove a most unusual success, despite the tragedy to do with your director. Such a loss."

"Yes," I said. "He couldn't have picked a more unusual time to die."

"This is the movie with the girl?" the gray man asked.

Marlet said, "Yes," and to me, "is Juju still on salary?"

"No," I said. "We've finished filming. We're done with the cast."

"Terrible about the director," the gray man said. "I understand it would have been a comeback for him?"

Marlet nodded vaguely. "He was a close friend?" he asked me.

"No," I said. "We've worked on projects, but never as close friends."

"Even so," Marlet said, "The shock—"

"It wasn't necessarily a shock," I said. "His drug problem was a kind of Russian roulette. I'm sure the precinct narcotics division are still investigating the death."

Marlet said, "Yes, I assume so. Such a talented man."

"Yes," I said. "He had a great deal of talent."

"We've been discussing the Vermond matter," he said. "And of course the girl... Henri–" that was the guy's name, "has been the thorn in our side, as one says."

"Oh?" I said.

"This business about the artist's condition," Marlet said. "I should say the dis*crepancies* that have a clear picture at bay. Won't you join us?"

"Please take my chair, sir," the man called Henri said, standing abruptly. He was very tall and thin. His mouth hardly moved. "I must hurry."

"You're leaving, Henri?" Marlet asked.

"I am late as it is," the man said. "Very nice to have met you, Mister Morgan. I will look forward to seeing this motion picture."

I shook his hand again and took the chair facing Marlet. "I was on my way to the office," I said. "They're in post-production and since Lajos' mishap I've been more directly involved–"

"I understand," the detective said. "But it is not particularly a coincidence my finding you this morning–"

"I didn't think it was," I said.

"Oh," he said with a smile, "it *is* a coincidence–purely a coincidence in that sense, though I've been looking forward to a brief chat with you. Do you have time now, sir?"

"About what do you want to chat?" I asked.

"Only hoping you might shed some light, let us say to put to rest a nagging situation." He motioned to the waiter, for more coffee. "Would you care for some coffee?"

"I've had coffee." I ordered a glass of wine. "What light might I shed on your nagging situation?"

"About the girl," he said. "Juju. I worry about her. She is such a rash young person–"

"They all seem that way from our side of the hill," I said.

"Of course, you're right. But Juju has this other side of her personality that seems, well, if you'll forgive me, she seems to attract a number of people that are–how do I put it? Out of her league?"

"An opportunist?" I said.

"Is that what you think?" he asked.

"She's actually very much like Mark Lajos," I said. "When he was younger, of course. He was more directly involved with films while the girl, well... She is young, as you say. But there is much in common with them."

"And with you, sir?" he aid.

"I don't know what she has in common with me," I said. "She perhaps sees me as a mentor or sorts."

"Yes," Marlet said, nodding, lifting his cup. "And no doubt more—"

"What do you mean?" I said.

"I'm saying no doubt there is more to your relationship with her than might seem instructional."

"Are you interrogating me?" I asked with a smile.

"No, oh, no! Forgive me if it seems like that! Certainly not! In fact, quite the contrary. I confess we are at a standstill on closing the Vermond matter, and quite sincerely have been hoping for your support."

"My support?"

"Your *help*", he said. "Your assistance in some of this. I'm only putting it this way because, well, knowing the girl as I do, I am assuming you have no doubt been intimate with her, and she with you, that and you have possibly shared some confidences. She is very excitable—"

"And also of legal age here in Paris—"

"Of *course*! What are you thinking?" he said. "I mean, after all, sir, you are a highly qualified and respected professional in your field, while Juju is—certainly to outward appearances, one of thousands of these children running around no doubt homeless on the streets. As I am sure they are everywhere—certainly Los *Ange*les. So you can appreciate, from an objective standpoint, that one viewing your relationship might conclude that it is, well—transient at best? You are going to Japan, are you not?"

I stared at him. "What sort of 'assistance' is it that you're looking for?"

He sipped his coffee. "It would be necessary for you to perhaps—" he paused, his mustache wet with coffee. It dripped as he chose his words carefully. "—perhaps—not necessarily be*tray* any confidences the girl has shared with you—but to perhaps *share* some *part* of these confidences with someone such as myself."

"She's told me very little about Vermond's suicide—" I said. "He was dead and she found him. She called the police."

Marlet smiled, shaking his head slightly. "I appreciate your honesty, and getting right to the point. But you see, the nagging situation is that we're not convinced Vermond's death was a suicide."

"Then what—?" I asked. "Murder? The girl hanged him? Possibly told me all about the bloody deed?"

Marlet fiddled with his spoon. "The inconsistencies—the discrepancies I mentioned, they are so blatant. You as a writer would be, I am sure, embarrassed to prepare such a scenario as Jean Paul Vermond's death. Such an amateurish set of circumstances can sometimes lead to far greater confusion than a carefully programmed execution of events."

I agreed. "So?"

"Let me lay my cards on the table," the detective said. I glanced at my watch. "Am I keeping you? I"m sorry," he said.

"No, go on," I said.

"Certainly Vermond was not 'hanged' by the girl. He was not 'murdered' by Juju, of course. But was she involved in some way or was she not involved? I'm situated as this juncture of speculation. It's conceivable at this point that she was a witness to what *did* occur. The timing is so acute—so infallible. She was *there*, you see."

I said, "She told me she found the body and notified the police."

"Yes, or course she did," he said. "That is a matter of record. Please understand I am not *persecuting* this girl as she has no doubt told you, and as she tells others. But I am praying that she will tell us about her brother—."

I must have looked shocked. He stopped talking as a series of almost imperceptible expressions coursed his face like a speed reel of an earthquake. "I don't know about a brother," I said. Ahhh, I could see Marlet smiling. Maybe Morgan wasn't as smart as he'd tried to be.

He stared at me for a long moment as those rapid reactions faded beneath a mask of suspiciousness. Now he *was* confused. He was the cop now. "Julian..." he said simply, almost reluctantly. "His name is Julian."

"I didn't know she had a brother," I said.

He look at me in disbelief. "No?" he said.

I shook head and some images sort of fell into place. The one following her—the potato head. Baggy, dirty coat and sunglasses. Some board under one arm. A shadow figure she threw rocks at. "But I think I know who you mean," I said. "A tall, dirty-looking fellow? Wears an old coat and carries a piece of board around?"

"It's a blackboard," Marlet said. "A child's slate board that he writes on with chalk. He doesn't speak."

"You mean he *can't* speak?" I asked.

"He's a mute," Marlet said.

"But he's the one that's stalking her—" I said.

"Oh, no," Marlet said. "He is not stalking her. He is stalking *you*, Monsieur!"

"Me?" I said. "What're you talking about?"

"Oh, my," he said, sighing. "From my perspective, you see, if one can prevent a crime before it is committed—"

"Wait a minute," I said. "You're trying to tell me this character that's following her around is actually following me? He's not stalking her?"

"He is following you," Marlet said. "If you see him—then he is following you. He has followed the girl to see who she is with, and then he will follow that person. I tell you, if I had any evidence I would arrest him. He would not be on the streets to follow *any*body!"

"And you're saying this person is Juju's *brother*, and possibly implicated in the artist's death?" Marlet nodded—not convincingly. "But you're not sure—" I said. "You've no evidence or proof... You're just speculating from your 'juncture'."

"Yes—except for the girl," he said. "I suspect she would be the witness to Vermond's death."

I didn't believe him. I wasn't sure what I believed. There was no way I wanted the detective following *me*. I had to find Juju. By the time the sun was gone I'd started looking for her. I took a cab from Leefeldt's to Saint Germain and walked back and forth. I wandered around rue Dauphine and walked past the gallery showing Vermond's work. Staring at the figures through the glass, I realized he had to have hanged himself. He'd seen it as a light in the dark narrow universe Juju'd told me he lived in. He'd raced towards that light. I stared at the figures in the boxes—the hanged men, the hanged artist, and I stared at the goddess in the box, her tangled plaster hair creating a Medusa of shadows.

Standing there for moments, I became aware of another reflection in the glass and I shrunk my depth of vision to the window in front of my nose.

He was behind me across the street, half-hidden in a black doorway—a curved wall sort of allowing his slouch into its chalky shape. The same coat—the same sunglasses. He didn't even look like Juju.

I had to find her and I walked slowly from the gallery window, heading towards rue Mazarine. Then I turned right, going in the direction of Beaux Arts. I stopped and looked around, but I didn't see him. Instead of going further, I walked back to Christine where it cut off of Mazarine. I started walking fast.

She'd left the black-walled flat sometime after we'd gotten out of the bed. Twice she'd changed the bandages on her stomach and her breasts, saying the marks were only scratches. Her body had flooded the scrapes with a thick, clear salve. There'd be scabs, she said. "I can pick the scabs off and it will leave marks—scars across me like they have been written on my body!"

I decided to head back down to Saint Germain, sort of going round in a circle, a squared-off angular path. I passed places I knew from the last movie. We'd shot on the Left Bank—against the stone walls I was strolling past.

By the time I was on Saint Germain again, I realized I'd lost the potato head. I headed slowly towards Boulevard Saint Michel, looking in the cafes, stopping to swallow several fast glasses of wine. The boulevard was crowded with people—many Japanese tourists, a dense movement of bodies like a rolling sea.

They were clotted under the big blinking neon over the door, a curling sort of figure eight—or a cowboy lasso spelling out *Red Egg*. Their faces, red from the glow, faded into gray with each wink of the lights.

The band blaring from the center of the room was surrounded with the same sea-sick motion of bodies circling them. It made me dizzy, sick as I squeezed through them hunting some sign of Juju. Some clutch of them had huddled off around two girls who'd taken everything off and were thumping and gyrating to the deafening beat stark naked. Neither was the one I was looking for. They were clawing each other, a couple of clothed arms holding the arms of one while the other thrust against her, running her nails down the girl's body and biting her neck and shoulders.

My stomach was rising inside my chest and I pushed and pressed myself through the crowd to the side stairs leading up to the alley between the buildings. They were even jamming together on the bottom steps. I had to climb over them—almost scale them to reach the alley.

Thinking I was going to throw up, I bent forward from the waist against the building opposite the Red Egg. But I wasn't throwing up. When I raised my face, I was looking down the narrow ribbon of dark alley to someone squatting or sitting against the wall, half showing in the yellow light from the top of the stairway.

I took a step deeper into the alley. It was Tanyous, his white shirt was muddied down the front. My shadow fell across him for an instant and I could see the whites of his eyes to the far side as he'd rolled them towards me. His face looked wet and he was moaning or saying something I couldn't hear above the music mercilessly vibrating against the walls of the buildings.

I straightened up and walked towards him. He was sitting with his rump in the trash and his back slumped on the wall. His arms were across his chest and his hands clutching his side. "You're Tanyous—" I said. He looked in pain. I asked, "Where is Juju tonight?"

He was staring up at me and tried to say something—opening and closing his mouth. A big bubble of saliva came out between his lips, broke and ran down his chin. I almost laughed, but then I saw it wasn't mud on his shirt but blood. There was blood on his pants and he seemed to be sitting in a small puddle of it. My first thought was Juju'd managed to cut him—part of the video or art thing that'd gone wrong.

"What's the matter with you?" I asked loud above the music.

It took him a moment to say it. "I have been shot, sir."

"Shot?" I squatted down, moved his arm and asked, "Where're you hit?"

"In the side... Here—" he said and moved his hand to his right side. I quickly unbuttoned his shirt.

"Jesus—" I said. "What the fuck happened?" He'd bled down into his pants and I could hardly see, but made out where the blood was coming from. A small hole an inch or two from his right ribs and towards the center of his chest. Maybe two inches below his right nipple. "Who shot you?" I asked, trying to ease his back from the wall but he groaned painfully. I put my hand around to his back, feeling for an exit wound but couldn't find one on his back. He was bleeding from his other side. I stood up and came around to his right and got down on my knees in the trash. "Where else does it hurt? Are you hurt anywhere else?"

He shook his head. Then I saw it—on his right side. Unless he'd been hit twice. "Were you shot twice?" I asked him.

He shook his head and tried to say he didn't know. Then he said, "No—one time... I think—"

"Has anyone called for help?" I asked. He shook his head. "Don't try to get up," I said. "Stay right there!"

I tried to get into the back door but couldn't, so I crossed the street to a bistro and called the police and an ambulance. When I hurried back into the alley, a girl was looking down at him. I said, "He's been shot—" She seemed to panic and pushed her way back into the Red Egg. In a moment, two or three others were in the alley, looking down at us.

I told Tanyous to sit still. "An ambulance is on the way. Who shot you?" I asked.

"It looked like he had a towel wrapped around his hand... I thought he had a cast...a broken arm... There was a flash and the...towel or cast exploded. I didn't hear much.... too much noise. Only like you...hit a wall with your hand. I felt like I was hit by a big board...it made me jump. So hard...like he hit me with a hammer—" He paused, grimacing. "I am going to die?"

"No," I said. "It looks like you've been hit once and the bullet came out over here under your arm. Have you got blood in your mouth?" He didn't know. "Are you in much pain?" He shook his head. That wasn't good. "I've called the cops," I said. "The ambulance'll be here in a minute—" I looked up at the others and yelled to be heard. "Get me a towel—get me a bunch of paper towels or napkins—" I put my hand behind Tanyous' back. "Just don't move," I said. "If you were only shot once then the bullet isn't in you, but are you spitting blood?"

He shook his head weakly. Someone offered a handful of napkins and I pressed them to the small hole in Tanyous side, placed his hand over it and wadded some others against the wound on his chest. He made a painful face and I thought he'd pass out.

"I came out to breathe," he said. "He was there...across the alley. The towel around his hand... He was in the dark—there. It was so fast..."

"Who was he?" I asked.

"I don't know..." he said.

"Where is Juju?" I asked.

He shook his head. "I can't hear you good..."

"Was Juju here—with you tonight?"

"No... I have been...working—" he coughed and there was blood on his mouth. I could hear the siren somewhere south of the Red Egg. "I think she went..." he seemed to be falling asleep. Then he opened his eyes wide. "I can't feel the pain this moment. Does that mean I will die, Monsieur Morgan?"

"No—" I said. "Just hold on—be still—" The blood was leaking quickly into the napkins. He'd lost quite a bit of blood. I felt I could stop it. "Give me something else!" I told some of the others. Someone had a scarf. I bunched the napkins and wrapped the scarf around Tanyous chest. "This might hurt—" I said.

"No...I am feeling nothing now...weak. I can't feel my hands."

"You'll be all right, Tanyous. Listen, you hear the ambulance? It's coming. Just keep your eyes open. Breathe low—you know, take shallow breaths. I don't know what's been hit inside. You're going to be okay. Talk to me—tell me who the guy was?"

"My vest is gone," Tanyous said. "I fell down. I called for help...a boy came in the alley but he pulled off my vest..." Tanyous' head dropped and his hands went limp, turning palms up. I felt his heart. It was beating fast.

"Can you hear me?" I asked. He couldn't hear me. I kept my finger on his neck, feeling his pulse.

I told someone to flag the ambulance into the alley. I tried to keep pressure on the wounds to hold back the blood, and kept feeling his neck to make sure his heart was still going.

Maybe fifteen minutes the attendants farted around without giving blood, and I was dumbfounded the boy didn't bleed to death in the alley.

They sped off to the hospital—a second-rate institution split up for an overcrowded psychiatric facility, and the next chance I had to break from Leefeldt's to stop by and see the boy was two days later. Inspector Marlet had been there at sunrise the morning after the shooting, and they'd had Tanyous half propped up in a kind of portable backrest. By the time I saw him he was in another wheelchair, smoking profusely and staring out the window in a glassed-in corridor off the ward. He seemed shocked to see me, pleased but greatly surprised. After thanking me for helping him, he said he was very nervous, very agitated. Afraid now the shooter'd be back to finish the job since he'd think Tanyous could identify him.

"Can you?" I asked.

"I told the police what happened to me and all I can remember. They did not seem so interested that I am nearly shot to death, but have come back twice to ask who did this to me. I don't know if I would recognize him. He had the dark glasses, and I was not seeing his face as much as that towel around his hand. That policeman says I am not cooperating, but I don't know what I can do?"

"You're quite lucky," I said. "There's not much damage considering you've got a hole through your body."

He sucked hard on the cigarette, then coughed. "Now I fear he will come back and stick an ice pick into my chest like that hit man was going to do in the old Steve McQueen movie. That's why I want to get out of here. Can you get me out of here, Monsieur Morgan? But you have done so much for me already. You have saved my life and I am in your debt."

"No," I said. "It was just one of those things..."

'Very strange,' Marlet had said, wondering how I happened to be on the scene and where was the girl? I avoided the detective whenever I could. Twice I'd seen him for moments—he'd appeared at the corner or getting out of a car just as I happened to walk past. "Yes!" I'd say. "I haven't seen her yet. I must hurry—the movie is in a mess—" which seemed something he understood.

They'd retrieved the bullet that'd passed through Tanyous, missing anything important. "Just a little this way or a little that way," Marlet said. "It could have struck a bone and gone down into his chest or upwards into his neck and his head. Who knows these things? It is the Russian roulette you mentioned about

Lajos's drug-taking." Tanyous told the police he hadn't been sure if a second shot was fired. There was just the wound from the one shot that had made a clean exit.

"Where's Juju today?" I asked Tanyous. Two days and I couldn't find her. When I wasn't in the flat I left the door unlocked so she could get in. She didn't show up.

A nurse at the hospital station had said she was there—she'd come in, spent some time with the patient, then left, only to return later with another boy. The nurse said, "They visited briefly."

Tanyous said, "They are shooting the video. Running around on the motorcycle. Maybe at Disneyland. She was supposed to come back but she hasn't. I am hoping Al will come and I can get out of here."

"When are they going to Disneyland?" I asked.

"Tonight—tomorrow—I don't know. They are running around while I am here with the police bothering me. If they go today, I won't be able to get out of here. Maybe you will see them on rue Dauphine and tell them to come back. You have not seen her?" I shook my head. "Please tell her to come back. He is crazy—Al. He thinks he is going to Germany. He has a letter from Berlin—about the film festival. It is not an invitation—only a letter—a form. But he is already talking about getting to Berlin—" He looked down and pushed his hand into the robe against his chest. "I am bleeding again!"

I called the nurse who wheeled him off, saying something about the drain in the wound. A certain amount of drainage was to be expected, she said.

He thanked me for coming and I reassured him, then left the hospital.

After seeing Tanyous, I didn't have very far to look for Juju.

She was with a half-dozen laughing film students lounging at the tables and two or three motorcycles in front of the cafe on rue Dauphine. I waved to her, calling her over. She wanted me to join her and the others. "No," I said. I took her arm gently and led her from the group. "I have to talk to you," I said.

She smiled and touched at her hair with a large green and red plastic styling brush. She came a few yards from the tables and stood in the shade of the awning where I asked her to break away and come back to the flat with me.

"Oh, no, I can't, Jake. We're going to Disneyland! I am going to skate when we get inside of Disneyland—around and around—"

"Juju, I said. "That's fine, but I've got to talk to you about what's been happening."

"Oh, yes," she said, blinking at me. "Poor Tanyous. He is all right, Jake. We were there and he will be okay."

"I know," I said. "I saw him earlier."

"They said he will be out of bed tomorrow and can walk with a cane because his left side is weak—"

"Yes—" I said. "But it's about—"

"You are the person that saved Tanyous," she said, "and everybody knows about this." She beamed. "You are a hero, Jake!"

"I'm not a hero," I said. "Listen to me, Juju. I had a talk with the police guy that tags around after you. He told me about what's been happening—about your brother—"

She looked as though I'd struck her on the face. I quickly told her about my encounter with Marlet and my surprise to learn she even *had* a brother.

"That little man has lied to you," she said, her eyes narrowing. "He is not talking about my *brother*! That person he is talking about is *not* my brother. He is a *half* brother and he is like a *weasel*—he wants money from me and that is why he follows me like a dog! So I chase him away! *Poof*! Go away, I tell him! Get away!"

"Why didn't you tell me that's who this person is?" I said. "Why didn't you tell me who you've been chasing away?"

"Oh!" she said. "And would you have told me you have such a monster following you around the city? Begging money and *stealing* from you! Would you say, 'Oh, Juju, and this is the person who says they are related to me—and they will follow us like a dog and *steal* from us.' Ha!" she said. "Who would tell someone such a thing?"

I said, "This detective believes he had something to do with your Jean Paul's death. He says you were there when Vermond was dead, and you know something—"

"Lies!" she yelled, then glanced around to others who were looking at her. "You are not supposed to be listening to me!" she told them. "Mind your business!" A couple of the motorcycles started up, and she had to raise her voice. "He has lied to you, Jake—"

"That's what this is about—and now there's been the attempt to kill Tanyous."

She looked oddly shocked. "No! Do you mean they think this weasel *shot* poor Tanyous?"

I stared at her. "Yes."

"No, that cannot be," she said.

"Even Tanyous describes him—" I said.

"Oh, so many clockards on the street. They all look like that—"

Maybe," I said, "but I think this cop thinks *I* know something that I don't—"

"There is nothing for you to know or anything for anyone to know because I have told everything there is about Jean Paul. This inspector does not know anything, and he is trying to bluff you into getting me into trouble with him. They do not know what they are doing and I can see this little man would bluff you into *betraying* me!"

"I have nothing to be*tray* you with," I said. "He isn't bluffing me—"

"But I can see there is doubt in your eyes and you believe him—"

"No!" I said. "I don't believe anything. How can I?" She started away and I took her arm. "Juju—please come with me. Don't go to Disneyland. *I'll* take you to Disneyland—"

"Al is doing the video and I am skating now—"

"Where is Al? Which one is he?" I asked.

"I am riding to Disneyland with Al because Tanyous is in the *hos*pital, Jake. We are working on the video and then maybe tonight we are going back to the Red Egg. I will telephone you—"

"Telephone me?" I said.

"So I can talk to you," she said. "How can we talk when the band is playing and everyone is making noise?" She stared at me. "Jake, I am going to be a performance artist. Al is going to film me with a *real* camera—a movie camera, and I can open the cuts I have. He told me these cuts will be scars and that I can open the cuts again—it will not hurt, and I can be a performance artist and will go on television."

"That's crazy," I said.

She pulled up the tee-shirt and showed me the red lines—more like deep scratches now, though she had a row of adhesive bandages covering half of her left breast.

"Juju—it's your *brother* or your half-brother or whatever you want to call him—he's the one the inspector thinks probably shot Tanyous—"

She was shaking her head. "Oh, no—that isn't right. I can see what they are doing. It is very wrong—no, Jake, you must not believe what they say."

"Then prove it to me—I don't want this cop hounding after me as well—" She suddenly pulled her arm away so sharply she almost fell over.

"I must go now, Jake—"

"Wait!" I said. "Don't go."

She waited. It was as though I was looking at a different person inside the body I recognized, someone else's eyes that were shining out. I didn't recognize her.

"Jake..." she said. "I will do anything for you, you know."

"Then come with me—" I said.

"I will do anything for you," she went on. "I feel that what I have of my soul is now in your possession. It is something that is greater than two people who fall in love. More mature than one young person claiming they are so in love with a girl. You understand what I am trying to say to you, Jake? It is my soul that is now in your possession."

"What are you talking about?" I said.

"I am saying it is the same as with Jean Paul, that he had my soul until he died. Now you have my soul, Jake. I have given it to you, and now I must go skate at Disneyland—"

"Wait!" I said. "Juju, it makes me sad that you are leaving right now. I mean it *troubles* me. I want you to be with me—to talk about Japan... "

"But I must go, Jake, my dear. I am leaving my soul with you. I told you that you now possess my soul and that nobody else can possess it as long you do. I am yours completely. Do you understand?"

"No. It still doesn't make you stay with me. To stay with me now—tonight. There's things we have to talk about After what we've experienced, I feel it is vital that you should stay."

"Your American brain is speaking," she said, smiling slightly.

"Perhaps that's it," I said. "But your detective is now breathing down my neck."

"I am yours," she said. "My soul is yours. It will be yours as long as you want to and no one else can possess it, Jake, my dear. It does not matter what others say or do or what I do, because that part of me now belongs to you for you to do with as you please..." She went up on her tiptoes and kissed me. She turned to the others, then looked back at me and made a sad, comic look. She climbed on the back of one motorcycle, and the driver—the slim, black-haired boy with sparkling teeth and eyes—gunned the engine. She threw her arms around his waist and the motorcycle roared away from the curb, the other bikes falling in line.

I must have walked miles. I hadn't walked as much since the gangster movie when I'd almost worn out a pair of shoes. Divi and I had walked the length of the river. The thought that I was carrying Juju's soul with me while she raced off to Disneyland on the back of Al's motorcycle was like I'd been handed a Zen koan. "Go figure, Jakey boy," I could hear Mark's smirk from his

Hungarian grave.

I stopped for a drink, had second thoughts about it, thinking I should sober up a little and get on with the Japanese script. But then I walked on and stopped in another bistro—another cafe, and had a quick glass of wine in each. In one, as I stood at the little counter, I caught my reflection in a sideways mirror, the glass up at my mouth and head bent down at it as though I were sucking it through a straw. A desperation in the face, some ancient man that had been put back together in his youth without fully throwing off the ages carried with him, so that time seemed hazed over him. It had indeed been a very long time since the submarine movie.

The ugly light was across my face, showing the pits and pores like bits of black powder. I quickly left from the cafe and kept walking.

Dark streaks of purple and black were smearing across the sky. The river was loud—calling out, it had a throaty continuous voice. I listened to its hollow, dark sound and watched figures in the grass of the little parks. A couple were hugging on sheets of spread-out newspaper. She had a white dress like a nurse's uniform.

I walked by the bridge before the Jardin Des Tuileries, slowly with the dark coming down, my thirst increasing. Past the Obelisque and north to rue Saint Honore, I stopped in a better cafe and ordered beef and a bottle of wine.

Gazing at the veins in the meat, I decided I couldn't eat and asked the waiter to remove the plate. I ate the bread and mustard and drank the wine, then ordered a glass of brandy and stared at the night street.

Walking slowly, a chill running over me, I went down to the Metro and got a first class ticket. The other classes were full up. I was almost alone in the train, looking back into the other packed cars.

Back on the Left Bank, I became gradually aware of something; an awareness like sensing the rise of a low-grade fever in one's system. I was being followed.

Two more blocks and I stepped into a corner bistro and

ordered a glass of wine. Leaning against the little green tile counter, I turned and stared out at the street. Just a glimpse, like catching something out of the corner of your eyes.

The sonovabitch was following me.

It looked as though he'd snuck around the side of a building. I left the drink and hurried around the next corner. It was starting to rain. The drops of water struck my face and spattered into my eyes. I quickened my pace—hurrying now. He stepped up his pace. I could hear him. Around the next corner I started to jog a little. The street was dark—narrow. I started doubling the pace. My chest ached. A stitch in my side almost bent me in pain.

Then I saw him: he was running—running funny, like a gangly scarecrow, his legs coming up high, the knees way up and legs reaching out as in a cartoon. It seemed to carry him quickly—lightly.

He was behind me and staying back, and then when I turned the corner ahead and kept going, he didn't show. That got me nervous. Had he dropped off? Had he cut through one of short alleys around the back of the building or underneath them or maybe flying overhead?

It wasn't until I reached the corner of rue Serpante and thinking maybe I'd lost him, when I saw him again—closer, he'd somehow snatched up the slack of distance between us and was heading directly towards me from the opposite direction. The dark coat was flapping like a grotesque cape and squinting into the rain, I could see he was wrapping a light colored towel around one hand, sort of swinging it in a circle, winding it around the hand.

Luckily I knew I'd make the building before he could reach me with that loping gait. I jumped down the steps and ran sharply past the horse meat shop to the old iron gate. Getting through it, I slammed it shut, throwing the lock and was just turning to the stairs when he was at the gate. He couldn't open it but that towel-covered hand jutted between the bars—like he was pushing a big snowball at me. I could see the tip of the gun—the round black hole nestled in the grimy towel like the eye of some bug or weird pet, and then it cracked. Not loud—just like a whip snapping. The feeling was like I'd been hit by a rock but nothing bounced—nothing hit the ground.

I was falling down as if I'd been shoved hard. I could see his grimace—the teeth were small and far-spaced, like they had black holes between them. I couldn't see the eyes behind the dark glasses. His cheekbones were like knobs, hard ridges, and his cheeks sunken in. Rag mop sort of ratty hair like an old Beatles cut or like the bangs of Moe in the Three Stooges.

He fired the gun again, but I didn't feel anything hit me. He'd missed the second shot that pinged off the stone steps and wall and hit somewhere up above me. Just a banging and a rackety sound in the stairway. I'd fallen down—the first shot had hit me on my side above the right hip—maybe it glanced and was like someone'd struck me with a bat.

Running away, his feet making loud splattering sounds in the rain water and I was wondering who the liar was who said you couldn't feel the bullet. Maybe they meant you couldn't feel the bullet because you were feeling the blow of it.

I found myself sitting down on the steps while the guy'd bolted onto rue Serpante and did a sharp turn running to the right past the building. I just saw the flapping shape of him heading into the rain.

What I was thinking was how stupid it all seemed—"Jesus Christ—Jesus Christ," I was saying to the wall, then pulled my shirt out of my pants. No pain in my arms, just my hip like I'd fallen down a flight of stairs.

The tail of my shirt on the right side was bloody and dark like there was mixed in the blood some almost black substance. Had the bullet burned me? I opened my pants and looked down into them at my side. It was as if somebody'd ran a gouge across my side—torn through part of my upper hip. Had it hit the bone? I couldn't tell. I felt nothing in my pelvis except a burning sensation that was reverberating with a sense of something having struck me with a great deal of force.

Grabbing hold of the iron rail, I tried to stand, pulling myself but I had no feeling in my right side from the waist down. My leg sort of crumbled under me. Shit! Shit, I said—the fucker'd hit nerves. Paralyzed the shit out me! One of my worst fears coming true!

The hole sort of curved in, pulling the skin into itself while the blood ran out steadily.

I couldn't stay there—I couldn't sit on the steps, and tried to get up again. I made it upright, and unlocked the gate with my key. Hobbling on the left foot because I couldn't feel the right, I gripped the wall for balance and made it out the gate and to the left to the horse meat shop.

Standing under the gold-painted horse head, I gave several solid raps on the glass before I felt myself sliding down as if I'd been suspended on strings that'd suddenly been cut.

Not for a moment had I thought I'd die, even as I vaguely heard the attendant say the word for "bleeder." He said, "This fellow is a bleeder..." Something I'd never known. As we seemed to be bumping along somewhere, I found myself hazily wondering back over the years to some of the accidents and mishaps where I'd drawn blood. I couldn't recall anything serious except—yes, when I'd cut myself, I seemed to bleed profusely until I'd stop it up somehow. I'd always just thought that was a healthy sign— good blood flow.

"If you had waited too long," a woman was saying, "you would have lost enough blood to fall into a coma." She made a clucking sound. They were injecting something into me, my arm reaching out to the side on the uncomfortable table.

I was out cold. For how long I didn't know, but awoke out of a glue-like sleep with my throat on fire. After a few moments of realizing I was in the infirmary, I remembered the vague movements of Eston, and Che Che stopping up the wound which I was told later wasn't a thorough bleeder, and though I wouldn't have bled to death on the steps, without proper attention I'd have joined Mark Lajos maybe within a day. So I was told by the doctor—the woman.

Inspector Marlet was quick to respond to the "gunshot" call, and almost in a state of shock to find me.

I remembered Eston—thinking at first I'd fallen because his mother said, "Oh, Morgan has fallen and hurt himself!"

Che Che said, "He hasn't 'fallen,' honey, someone's plugged him with a shot."

"A shot? A shot?" they were saying. I couldn't remember the car. Yes, then I did: the dinky Fiat of Paul's. The dented hood and broken windshield. His hunched back was in the way. They practically folded me into the car and Paul drove bent over the wheel, twisting it with both hands. There wasn't room for anyone else in the car. They took a cab—racing close behind Paul's Fiat. It was like a party, Che Che said at the infirmary. "We should've brought Mark here."

Eston said, "He was dead, Che Che. You leave a body where it lays."

I don't remember the doctor cauterizing the wound.

I ached. The bullet had broken a piece of bone off and lodged in the fatty skin on the right side.

It was a .32. Miserable fucking shot. He hadn't killed Tanyous and he hadn't killed me. Of course we both could've died. Tanyous had been a matter of minutes. I'd saved his fucking life.

Marlet said, "It seems your assailant fired point blank without hitting you, Mister Morgan. It appears you were hit by a ricochetting bullet. The second shot was wild as well."

"We're dealing with a gunman who can't shoot straight," I said.

"This is because Julian Mostrom—that is his name—is practically blind."

"A blind gunman," I said. "It was Julian, I have no doubts. He was as close to me as you are." I shifted on the bed. "Is that the girl's name—Mostrom?"

Marlet shrugged. "The mother was the same, I believe. Her

name was not Mostrom. Julian's father was Antonio Mostrom. He was an artist—an illustrator, and a writer of sorts. This information, of course, comes from our initial inquiries of the girl following the Vermond situation. None of it has been verified because there are so few facts to do with either of these people. Needless to say, we are looking for both of them."

"What has she to do with his shooting people?"

"Perhaps conspiracy? It is not your mishap or the attempted murder of the Iranian that we're interested in as far as the girl is concerned. It is very important that we find her and the brother—half-brother—because of the pressure to do with Vermond's death."

If Eston's mother hadn't been in there with her hands dripping horse meat, I'd have stayed beneath the window and bled into a coma.

Shortly after Marlet hurried off, Robert appeared with a bunch of papers for me to sign. He told me the police had been to the office, bothering the godfather. Beneath his unruffled facade, Leefeldt was freaking. "All of this has to do with Juju," Robert said, shaking his head. "It is all my fault—I brought her to the godfather."

"Then it's his fault," I said.

"But I vouched for her," Robert said. "There was no way of knowing—in fact there was nothing to know about her. She never talked about this person—this one that shot you and Tanyous."

Eston showed up to take pictures, and said, "I let our girl in the gate. She went up to your flat."

"Is she there now?" I asked.

He didn't know. "She showed up after the cops left—they dug a lot of holes in the downstairs and pried off some plaster. They're out looking for guy that plugged you, Jake."

I tried phoning my own apartment but the line was busy. A few hours later I called Eston and told him to go up and check it out. He called me back and said the phone was off the hook—laying on the bed. The girl was gone. He said, "The fucking place looks like it's been burglarized, Jake."

The typewriter was gone. Some jewelry I never wore was gone. I'd left some francs and a mountain of coins and those had been taken. What bothered me was the Luger. That was gone. So was the clip and what shells I could find. One was still in the box. The lid for that was under the bed.

I didn't know where Tanyous lived—he was still in the hospital but she'd probably gone to his place—with Al. I figured she'd been there and hit my flat with Al or his pals. She'd had to have opened the door.

Moving as best I could, I grabbed a cab and headed down rue Dauphine. Then I went to the Red Egg.

The air was blue with smoke and the stink of crack; a deadness to the music like the steady beating on the bottom of a wash tub. Most of the girls in black and their faces white.

Other tight-packed faces sweating in a kind of ritual spinning around like dervishes. Nuts. I made my way to the back and stood stuffed against a corner wall; I drank and smoked but I couldn't bring the cigarette to my mouth at moments—the back of someone's head inches from my face. I started to move, to lean sideways through the crowd—my hip aching. My leg felt like my knee was coming apart.

Then I saw him. He was tall enough to be half a head above the others and he didn't have the glasses on. He was squinting so severely his eyes were just puckered slits. His face was sick looking and dense as a pinball. Sweat was leaking down his face from under the weird clump of hair—he looked like Moe in the Three Stooges or an early Beatles maniac. His cheekbones were like knobs, hard ridges, and his cheeks sunk in. He didn't look anything like Juju—though he was supposed to be her half brother, some genes had to filch through somewhere. Nothing showed on him. He angled right, that black board wedged under one arm and the hand in the pocket of that ratty coat—it was long and black, maybe a dirty charcoal—maybe wool, a tear in the vent at the rear, the hem dirty. One shoe was untied—some dirty tennis shoes. He walked on the lace with his other foot.

He went to the right around the corner into that alcove that opened to the toilets. I lost sight of him. I moved through the crowd and then turned the same corner and faced the greasy wood of the men's room door.

I opened the door and stepped in, letting it shut behind me. The smell was bad. A stretch of gray-painted concrete floor, and a couple of walls sticking into the room at angles. Past that was the shit holes. I imagined he'd gone to the shit hole because to the left were two sinks and two fags were pressing to one another before the dirty mirror. One started pissing in the trough next to the sink and looked at me. I looked past him and stepped on the cigarette, then walked for the shit holes. The door on the wall had a lock on it—a store room. The wall ended in a sunken area with two holes side-by-side in the floor to squat over. Orange footprints had been painted on the floor beside the holes.

He was squatting over the far hole. He'd gathered one side of the coat up on that leg, and was hunched down, his pants down on his thin thighs. He was scribbling on the chalkboard, the chalk squeaking on the dull black slate.

Then the board dropped, hit the floor and the slate split into pieces. I was startled, and then his face was turned towards me; his eyes no longer hard pinched holes, but were flashing like a wild dog's. The hand that'd dropped the slate was into the coat pocket and by the time I reached him and kicked at him, he'd whipped out the gun. I kicked him somehow on the shoulder and he fell to the right, the gun hand outstretched to catch himself and one shot went off, snapping and hitting the wall.

I grabbed that arm to get the gun and he slugged me with his other fist, banging me on the side of the head. I saw stars. His legs kicked to get a grip on the floor but his pants tangled his movements. He was strong. I had his wrist and I felt all the sinews in his arm as though he hadn't any skin. The smoke of the shot was burning my nose and the gun went off again. A section of mirror over the sink shattered and he was twisting the gun upwards to plug me in the neck or face. I wrenched at him hard—trying to rap his hand on the floor but he was too strong and the gun seemed glued to him. All I could do was jerk it up—then down, and then when he thought I'd try to slam him down, I jerked his arm up and it sprang against his chest. I had my hand or part of it between the hammer and the pin—I could feel it biting me bad.

His coat was bungling up, entangling both of us. I got a bunch of it up and over his face, covering his hand and the gun and my grip on him. I wanted to smother him but he loosened the tension and his right arm bent back to twist the gun around. With my side going numb, I pushed his arm up and though the gun was grazing my face I angled it around.

I tore my hand back, feeling my skin rip in that second when the hammer hit the pin. The blast deadened in the tangle of coat but the bullet fired into him and I saw a big vein in his neck swell up and pump up like a fat worm. Then it stopped and he shuddered. His piss spread across the concrete.

He was limp and I pulled the coat away and saw he'd been shot in the face, somehow in the upper jaw and into one nostril. Blood was coming out of the back of his head.

I stood up shaking, the shot was still reverberating in the dank room.

I turned around. Some faces were crowding at the opened door, peeking in. "He tried to shoot me," I said. "He's dead."

For most of the night I was in a chair at the police precinct. It was hard to believe. The worst was I needed something to drink. Desperately. I tried not to let it show. I thought back to the movie extra I'd shot, and seeing him a few I times around town. He always gave me a terrible look and backed away or made a quick exit as if I intended to shoot him again.

Marlet said, "I do not understand you, sir. I simply do not understand how this could have happened."

"We happened to bump into one another in the Red Egg," I said. "I went there looking for the girl. I guess he couldn't see me at first."

"This is very difficult," he said. I was asked to remain, until the two faries confirmed that the dummy'd pulled a gun and I'd kicked at it. They'd seen him before.

"A rotten person," one said. "He's a trouble maker."

Julian had been in the bar, scribbling on the chalkboard. One said he thought the dead guy lived with a Cuban queen—a fat female impersonator but didn't know where they lived.

I told Marlet I'd had to fight for the gun to save my life. "If I didn't, I wouldn't be sitting here now. It was an accident—the gun going off, but I can't say I'm sorry because he was getting the best of me."

Exhausted, in pain, arriving back at the flat by cab, I limped along the walk to the iron gate which I found hanging open. Mail was scattered on the steps and as I bent to pick it up, my stomach squeezed at the sound of feet shuffling quickly on the steps above me. I was barely able to straighten up when Claude seemed to lunge as if he'd tripped somehow and was flailing his arms for balance. Instead he was grabbing me.

"You son of a bitch!" he yelled, his face twisting into a bulldog's. "You rotten no good son of a bitch! Screwing my wife behind my back!" He flung himself on top of me and I went down onto the steps. Immediately sharp pains shot through my hip. "Why don't you die!" he cried. "I wish you were dead!"

We struggled, rolling down a couple of steps, and I was thinking that he must've sent Julian to try to kill me. But it didn't make sense. His breath was a fuming heat of rage and onions and booze.

He tried to strike me in the face but missed and his hand hit the wall. More plaster fell away. The wall was riddled with little holes the police had burrowed. Claude's hands were around my neck.

"Divi! My Divi!" he was crying as he tried to choke me and I struggled to crawl out from under his blubber.

The gate banged against the wall and hunchbacked Paul was coming at us. He looked wild, his teeth set. He swung his fist downwards, landing a hard, thudding blow between Claude's shoulders. With a huge gasp, Claude twisted up slightly, his hands dropping from my neck. He'd been winded and was trying to gasp when I struck him in the stomach. I followed it with another blow, and he rolled off. Paul took a side step and kicked at Claude. "You fool!" he shouted. "You stupid, ugly buffoon!"

Taking my arm, Paul helped me around Claude, writhing on the steps. "Are you all right, Jake? You're bleeding, man—"

I limped out and Paul pushed the gate. I saw his Fiat on the street and the Swahili girl in the passenger seat. "I better take you to the infirmary," he said.

"No, it's okay," I said. "I need a drink. Let's get a drink—"

"We can't all fit in the car," He said. "You remember that, don't you? I thought you'd fucking die on me."

The girl got out of the car and was standing a foot taller than me. She was lean like a rake but her firm breasts reached out boldly from the slim chest into two tender points. She said something in Swahili and he answered her—concerned. She looked worried. Her teeth were like bright flashes of light and her gums were a vivid red. She took my arm. Her long fingers wrapped around my forearm.

"She says you look weak, Jake," he said.

"I'll be okay—" I said. "There's a cafe at the corner..."

She said something else. "She says you're bleeding down your pants," he said.

"That fucking Claude—"

"No, it's that fucking Che Che bitch. She told him you'd been screwing Divi who's hiding out and putting a lean on old Claude..."

"Fuck him," I said. "I need a drink—" I looked up at the girl. She was beautiful. All kinds of jewelry wound around her long neck. She looked like she'd stepped right out of National Geographic. She put her arm around my shoulder and I let my head drop against her chest. I wanted to put my head on a breast but things got blurry–fuzzy. It was like I couldn't feel the sidewalk under my feet, only the sensation of those hands on my neck like some kind of hooks trying to get inside of me. I said, "Nobody can get inside of me–" and everything went black.

The pungent odor of smoke and ash hung in the hall. Marlet and I walked past Eston's then climbed the steps, the cop breathing heavy at my back, up to the burned flat. The stairway was filled with light from the opened, partly charred door. A hole the size of a bathtub had burned through the ceiling and roof and I was looking at the pale clouds. Moving ever so slightly, they had a crystal cleanness, an almost blinding diamond clarity. I'd had nothing to drink for the two days I'd been in the infirmary. Marlet and another detective had escorted me into a police car that morning. The inspector had seized my passport.

The skylight was blackened from smoke. One section had shattered which Marlet said was caused by the heat. "The fire was right here," he said, standing in the black debris where the big chair had sat. There was little left to salvage. "Gutted," he said in the car. "Your apartment has been stripped by the fire."

I stepped over the scorched metal of the bed and the wet lump of wood and ash that'd been the chair. Turning, I looked up at the sky–the sun pouring in through the roof. With my face into the light, I closed my eyes. Little red lines moved against my eyelids.

"What are you thinking, Mr. Morgan?" Marlet asked.

"I don't know what I'm thinking," I said. "Everything's burned. I've lost my wardrobe. How did the place catch fire? How did it start?"

"You don't know?" he asked.

"No!" I said. "I don't think I know... I don't remember it happening. I have–I have a vague..." I was staring down at the chain on the charcoaled floor by the bed.

His gaze followed mine. "A vague what?" he asked.

I said, "Some commotion. Was there anyone hurt in here?"

"Why don't you tell me," he said. "Surely you must know if there was someone in the flat."

I shook my head. "I don't know. I wasn't here. I'm only having a faint recollection of when I left—and some commotion." The stairs. I remembered Claude's red face. He'd grabbed my shoulders and then my neck. Paul had hit him. I didn't say anything to Marlet. He was bending over, with difficulty, and stuck the sharp point of a pencil into the handcuff. It was attached to the chain on the bed, and he raised it slightly.

"Was there someone injured in here?" I asked. "Is that why you've brought me here?"

He didn't answer, but poked around at the piles of ash. It appeared that part of the skylight had somehow exploded. Charred chunks of the glass with the burnt wire ends curling out of its sides seemed scattered over the area. That hole where the ceiling had fallen in—above the chair. The fire had burned upwards, roasting the building right between the narrow beams.

Marlet straightened up and stood very close to me. I could smell his breath. He looked at me carefully and I stared right back into his bulbous eyes. "You don't know, do you?" he said. I shook my head. "You were in the hospital and you don't remember what happened here?"

"No," I said.

He sighed. "Juju was not in this room when the fire occurred," he said. "But you must understand I am making an assumption—"

"Very well," I said.

"If Juju had been in this room—a prisoner, so to speak, and unable to free herself, of course she would be dead from the fire. Am I right?"

"You're the one making an assumption," I said.

"And so if she was dead by the fire and you were not here but were passed out in a drunken state on some train, then you would have no information on this occurrence?"

"Was she or wasn't she in this room?" I asked. I could see it now—in my head. She hadn't been back in the building since I'd been out of the infirmary. Claude lit the fire. Perhaps she'd popped in while he was starting his fire.

"If I told you the girl was dead," Marlet said, "would that refresh any memories you may have of how this fire started?"

"I wouldn't believe you," I said. "Is she dead?" He was just staring at me. Watching my face. I asked again: "Well, are you telling me she's dead?"

"Yes," he said. "The girl is dead."

I didn't know if I believed him. "How did she die?"

"She was shot," he said.

"Shot..." I said. "I don't believe you. Who shot her?"

"That is the mystery," he said.

"And you're suggesting I've had something to do with all this?"

"It would simplify matters," he said. He shrugged generously and motioned with his hands. "That is what we are trying to get to the bottom of."

"But you're fairly certain I'm the guilty party somehow," I said.

"The bullets that killed her—"

"Bullets? More than one?"

"The bullets had not been fired from the same gun that Julian used on the Iranian and on you. She was killed by a 9mm shell. The same kind of shell we found in this mess."

"That gun..." I said. "Do you have it?"

"We do not have any such gun," he said. "We have learned that you had a German luger when you were at the hotel."

"Yes," I said. "It was a 9mm. It was fairly valuable. I had shells for it."

"We have gone over all this carefully but haven't found such a gun. It is not in your belongings—we have checked carefully. Was the gun in your possession the day before yesterday?"

"What day was that?

"Wednesday," he said.

"No. The gun was missing when I came back here from the infirmary. It was here before I was shot."

"And what happened to this gun?" he asked.

"I don't know," I said. "I'd been leaving the door open while I was out. Last time I saw it was on the table over there—well, where the table had been. It was on the table at the base of the lamp." I was suddenly feeling hazy—almost dizzy. I said, "I don't believe the girl is dead. I don't believe the story you've just told me."

He nodded, then sighed heavily. "I need you to come with me, Mr. Morgan."

"Am I under arrest?" I asked.

"Oh, no, no," he said. "I need you to identify the girl. We will go to the morgue where you can see the girl's body."

"All right," I said, feeling I was about to call his bluff. It was absurd, of course. He had no reason to lie about such a thing.

We walked carefully over the fire debris. I could see now that they'd looked through the rubble—the ash, the hunks of charred, broken bits of stuff. I had no clothes except what the police had in my suitcase, in their car. In the bathroom, the walls were smudged black. The plastic handle of my razor was melted. The blade was black.

As I followed the inspector downstairs, he said, "We are not arresting you, Mr. Morgan, but I must advise you that we are holding your passport momentarily— until some of the vagueness of this situation clears somewhat..." I said I understood.

Past Eston's door and down the second flight, Marlet hesitated, puffed and caught his breath. He complained about pains in his legs. He said, "I am too old for all of this."

At the car, I asked, "Where is my suitcase?"

"Your baggage has been placed in the trunk for safekeeping."

The other detective nodded. "Unfortunately, we will need to examine your clothing a little further. It is a routine matter, Mr. Morgan. I would like nothing better than to see that you are in the clear." We climbed into the backseat and he lighted up a cigar. "Personally," he said, "you do not strike me as a man who would kill. Despite the violent and gruesome subject matter of your motion pictures." He blew out a cloud of smoke. "Of course, one can always be wrong," he said.

"Meaning I'm a good suspect," I said.

"In your situation," he said, "the drinking—the inability to remember events— even *days*, Mr. Morgan, or who you have been with and who you have not been with. You can appreciate the difficulties such behavior presents."

We said nothing more in the car until we got to the morgue, pulled into a narrow parking facility and walked down a long descending corridor into the basement. It seemed to be a spacious level beneath the administration. I began to feel queasy—weak almost, a terrible heat generating in my chest and stomach. Marlet could see my discomfort and took my arm, guiding me off the main corridor, down some narrow steps and through another doorway.

He spoke to an attendant as we continued down a hall past several large-wheeled gurneys supporting sheet-covered bodies.

"Here," Marlet said. "Stop here, Mr. Morgan—" I realized I'd walked as if in a trance. He turned me to the left and through an opened door into a narrow gray room. "I apologize for the informality of this," he said. "You understand we have not transferred her yet, although she has undergone a preliminary autopsy here."

"Oh..." I said.

We stopped in front of another gurney, another body under a sheet, smaller, more like a child's. Marlet nodded to the attendant who pulled back the sheet in an almost whipping motion that reminded me of a bullfighter sailing his cape to the air.

Juju was lying on her back with her eyes half open. I nodded. "I believe you."

"You are identifying her for the record?" he said.

"Yes. That's her. That's Juju. You could at least close her eyes—" I reached up and touched the cold face, moving my fingers to her eyes and lowering the lids. They came back up slightly, would not close completely. They felt rubbery. The smell of chemicals, of

Marlet's cigar cupped in his hand, and the odor of death was overpowering. I turned away. "She's shot in the head," I said.

"Yes," Marlet said. "At pointblank range. The one in the head killed her but she was shot twice again. Once in the throat—the bullet lodged behind her left shoulder blade—"

"I think I'm feeling sick," I said. "She's dead. I believe you. What the fuck more do you want? This is grotesque—"

"But please, understand the necessity—" he said.

"I do. That's fine," I said. "Let's get on with it."

"I understand," he said. "But please look at something, Mr. Morgan—" I turned around and stared at her body again. "These superficial lines—these are cuts to her abdomen and breasts and elsewhere—which occurred quite recently before her death. They are unrelated to her death, you understand."

"She made those marks on herself," I said.

"With—?"

"A corkscrew, It has a blade in it. A small knife blade."

He nodded. "Do you want to got to the washroom?" he asked. "Perhaps to freshen up?"

"Yes," I said. We left the room, Marlet's hand on my arm. "What do we do now?" I asked.

"Do?" he said. "What do you mean?"

"What happens now?" I asked.

He held open the washroom door for me. I ran the cold water, splashed it over my face. Marlet lit his cigar again and took several puffs. "The body must be claimed. Since she was a friend of yours... Otherwise she will be disposed of—"

"No," I said, bunching up a wad of paper towel. I shook my head. "I'll make arrangements. What do I do?"

"You will sign for it before you leave here. The arrangements you make will take care of the rest of it." I nodded. He drew in a mouthful of smoke and the end of his cigar glowed red. "Why did she cut herself in such a manner, Mr. Morgan?"

"She enjoyed it," I said.

"You are saying she was in your presence?"

"Yes."

"And you did nothing to stop her?"

"No," I said, dumping the paper towels in the trash. "I didn't stop her."

"I see," he said.

I looked at him. "*Do* you?"

Nodding slowly, thoughtfully, he said, "Yes, Mr. Morgan... We can take care of the paperwork here, and I'll have you delivered to the hotel—the Rond-Point de Longchamp, I presume?"

I said yes. On the way out, I asked, "Just how seriously am I considered a suspect? I mean even half-assed thinking that I'd somehow do such a thing to Juju is totally insane."

"Ah," he said, "but it is not possible at this point to weigh such a question accurately. These things have a way of presenting themselves, of declaring, as it were, their own sense of weight. But, technically, you are more of a suspect now than you were twenty minutes ago."

I just stared into his round, expressionless eyes. He wasn't smiling.

Pinaud was waiting for me that evening at the mortuary, wringing his hands. His face beaded with sweat. The soft fleshy throat spilled over the ridge of his collar, cinched up by the broad, dark flowered necktie. Late that afternoon, the mortuary had received the girl's body. He wanted to know my intentions and I said, "You can cremate her."

"I see," he said. "And what considerations have you made for inurnment, Mr. Morgan?"

"I don't believe there was anything mentioned like that," I said.

"The mausoleum—" he stated to say, but I held up my hand.

"No," I said. "She was interested in being cremated. Personal arrangements, you understand. What do you put her in afterwards?"

"There's several options," Pinaud said. "It depends chiefly on whether you will be keeping the cremains or disposing of them in some way. A fairly inexpensive mausoleum arrangement—"

"No," I said. "I'll take the ashes. A personal burial."

"I see. Yes..." he said, pulling a white handkerchief from inside his jacket and mopping his face with it. "This has all been very tragic. Jean Paul was my dearest friend—"

"Yes," I said. "I'm sure it has been upsetting."

"That Inspector has interviewed me, monsieur. He expressed much interest in what you and I might discuss. He knows, you see, that I happened to be acquainted with the girl and was actually responsible for introducing her to Jean Paul—to serve as a model."

"I can't see that we're having much of a discussion to relate," I said.

"May I show you some of Jean Paul's paintings?" he asked.

"No," I said. "I've no interest anymore."

"But about the piece that you were about to purchase," he said. "The goddess figure?"

I looked at him.

He said, "I'm willing to pay considerably for it—" he said. "You could make a handsome profit. I am sure that is important to you, but I am a collector, and Jean Paul's work—with things such as they are... I am afraid there will be a sensation of interest. I am told you are going to Japan?"

"Yes. If I can get my passport back. I'm a suspect in the girl's death—"

"No!" he said. "That's preposterous!"

"I agree. But the police would like me to stay longer. They believe I have some idea about Vermond's death that perhaps the girl conveyed to me. Maybe they're convinced I've had something to do with her murder, and frankly—I can't remember whether I did or not—"

"Oh!" he said, blustering. "Yes, they suspect anyone—including myself, which is equally preposterous. Of course, I don't believe you had anything to do with what happened to Juju Rhoda—"

"That's the first time I've heard anyone use her last name."

He smiled, wetting his lips. "That was what she called herself, monsieur. I don't know what her legal name was. Jean Paul told me she took the name from the back of a legal pad–the brand of the legal pad."

"She told me about the silver shoes," I said.

"The shoes...?" he asked.

I nodded. "The shoes and the coffin."

He looked pale and didn't say anything. His neck was getting red. I said, "When will you actually cremate her body?"

"It will be tomorrow after one o'clock. There's a certain procedure to do with the process."

"How long does it take?" I asked.

"Two to three hours for the preparation–"

"No, I mean the cremation itself."

He was nervous. Taking a deep breath, he said, "That is usually–well, I can't say exactly as it depends on the deceased. In this case, I would say less than one hour."

"I understand there is some corrugated container or cardboard?"

"That would be the most expedient," he said. "And the cremains? I presume–"

"I meant what do I carry them in? Isn't there some kind of take-out box?"

"Yes," he said. "There is a container–it is simply a box about this size–" he showed me with his hands. "It is a plain cardboard container–unless you wanted to have them shipped–"

"No," I said. "She wanted to be dumped in the river."

Pausing for a moment, he then smiled slightly. "I have children," he said. "My wife has been ill for some time, Mr. Morgan. For a very long time. In fact, she is practically an invalid... This other matter you mentioned–shoes–silver–"

I nodded. "At the morgue the girl was on a table. She didn't have any clothes on."

"We have–" he said, "a simple material. It covers the deceased. It is not a gown but–basically a wrapping that can be used if the decision is made to forego a cremation casket..."

"But a casket isn't necessary," I said.

"No," he said. "Of course, the use of such would lengthen the actual cremation time. There is another container—a larger—box situation. It is corrugated paper, in fact—"

"That's fine," I said.

"She would be covered when placed into the retort—"

"By this container?" I asked.

"Yes. It incinerates immediately."

"I'd like to see her now," I said, "if that's convenient."

He hedged a little. "I don't think that is an unreasonable request," He said. "However, her body is not covered at this moment. The police department—"

I nodded. "I saw her already. I'd like to see her again."

"If you will follow me, please," he said.

He opened the door to an adjacent room and that was a display room for caskets. Past this room we entered another with pews and a smaller square door in the far wall. "This is our chapel," he said. "Services are held here..."

I followed to the rear of the chapel and through another door. We were in an anteroom room like a concrete-floored garage with a kind of sunken center. The interior of the oven was visible for viewing the cremation. To the right along a platform were several small refrigerator style doors. Pinaud looked at me and said, "Juju is in this first compartment, Mr. Morgan." He hesitated.

"Well, you can open it up," I said.

He was looking at me. "If there is anything I can do for you, Mr. Morgan... I am sorry this terrible thing has happened, but—"

"There's nothing you can do for me, Pinaud." He stared at me for a moment then turned abruptly to the door and lowered the handle. It was like a closet and she was on a metal table, slid feet first into the narrow space. I could see the top of her head, her hair. Pinaud touched a switch on the outside wall and the little room was lit by a dull overhead single fluorescent tube. He frowned, stepped back and moved to one side.

I took the couple steps into the closet and stood to the side of the metal wheel table on which she lay naked in about the same position as at the morgue. Pinaud said, "If you'd care to have a small service, tomorrow morning—"

"No," I said, looking at her. "That wouldn't do any good." Her eyes were still half open. Expressionless and dark. "But maybe you could get that covering for her now," I said. "Something to cover her with?"

"Of course," he said. "I'll get someone to attend to it immediately." I was aware of Pinaud walking away quickly as I reached down and touched her face. I traced one of the scabbed knife scrapes with my finger, then bent over and kissed her forehead. I couldn't smell anything—no chemicals. Just the cool smell of a carefully swept garage. I lowered my face again and put my lips on hers. "Goodbye, Juju," I whispered, kissing her again. Her lips were cold and unyielding. It was the same as when I'd been a boy and kissed a store window mannequin.

I was touching only the shell of Juju. She'd passed her soul to me. That's what she'd said.

The godfather's lawyer, Raul, talked to the cops who it seemed had sat around wondering what I'd done with the gun after shooting the girl. That was easy—you toss it in the Seine! It sinks to the bottom never to see the sun again. The police were not leveling charges against me for the moment.

I was in Leefeldt's office—a wide ultra-modern or high-tech room with something like cushioned chrome smokestacks for seats. His desk chair towered above the visitors, like it had a chromed top a couple of feet above the godfather's head. He was a dark complected man, a deep olive color and a nose like a parrot's. The small hands were moving a gold-plated bi-plane across the desk in little forward and backward motions. He said, "Jake, you are the most valuable one we have today. Is there any truth to all of this confusion?"

"Except that I was wounded by this nut and ran into him in a can a few days later where he was ready to plug me again. I'm still all busted up from the battle."

Raul, the attorney, leaned forward from his smokestack. "The only question, it seems, is why did you go into the men's room after this character instead of immediately notifying the police? He was already wanted in connection with the shooting of that boy...?"

"I don't know," I said.

"You knew he might shoot again?" Raul asked.

"Perhaps fatally–outright?"

"Oh, I suppose so. I don't think there was any doubt. I've wondered about that–supposedly he couldn't see worth a shit. Maybe he was afraid of shooting us in the face. I've visualized his features up close and those glasses. I can see the magnification of them–strong, very strong. I can see the lenses but I can't make out the eyes."

"Hmmm," Raul said. "Still..." He didn't finish. We sat in silence for moments until Leefeldt cleared his throat.

"Yes, yes," he said. "An odd assortment of characters you apparently merged with."

"No odder than what I've been used to," I said. He smiled–a crinkling of his mouth like a Santa Claus.

"But you do not have any information on how this young woman was killed–the girl, I mean?" he asked.

"No," I said.

"It's incredible that we've lost two people associated with the production," Raul said. "Both by terrible deaths. It's as though–"

"Then we will push ahead with this," Leefeldt said quickly. "Clear this up for you to proceed with Hiromi. For now, Raul will be representing you, Jake, and you should not be bothered by the inquires–"

"However," Raul said, "This inspector has asked to meet with Jake informally–personally. He claims he wants to share some information with you," the lawyer said.

"I don't mind," I said. "I have nothing to offer him, though."

"I think that's fair enough," Leefeldt said, the little gold plane taxiing into a position alongside the massive desk pad. He flicked one of the propellers with his fingertip. The meeting was finished.

Marlet ordered a salad and licked his lips over some section of dressing. He said, "As any fool can see, I am overweight—unlike you. My cholesterol is not to be believed and as much as try I can't seem to shift them all around—the good ones and the bad." He chuckled a little. "It is much like my job, Jake—do you mind if I call you by your first name?"

"No," I said. "I feel we're like distant relatives."

"Well put. But to the bad and the good, Jake—you must understand, it is not this girl particularly—this poor Juju that is our real concern."

"No?" I said.

"Her case is an open homicide, of course. She was shot. Murdered. More than once suggests some other emotions involved..." He opened his brief case and brought out several photographs. "These are from the scene, Jake. The apartment where we found her body is south of here. Several miles. On the way to the Orly airport, as a matter fact."

"I have never seen this place," I said, my gaze on the dirty, cluttered linoleum, on the stacks of opened garbage bags against a wall. Everything seemed thrown about—ransacked. Smudges, stains on the wall. To the right of the bags was a filthy sink, the cabinet door at the floor scuffed from being kicked shut. Juju was on the floor on her stomach, her head turned right with her left cheek on the linoleum. Her right arm angled up, the hand not far from her face—the wrist turned at an awkward angle and the palm open, as were her eyes—fixed sightless along the level of the floor. Blood had pooled considerably about her in a large kidney shape—showing black in the photo. She'd bled from the side of her face on the floor, and from the mouth—partly open in the shot—the row of small teeth darkened by the blood. The tee-shirt was soaked and blood had seeped into the jeans.

To the left of her lower body the metal legs of a kitchen table reached into the picture.

I handed him back the photo—he had others—other angles of the body. "I don't want to see any more of them," I said.

"I am sorry," he said, slipping the file back into the briefcase. "You were never in that apartment?"

"No."

"It has only two rooms. And a hall—you can see the hall in one of the other photographs."

"I'm not interested," I said.

"There's several posters on the walls of the hallway," he said. "They advertise the Club Bivouac—a night spot for transvestites and impersonators—comedians, you see. The posters all show a fat, Samoan person—a female impersonator. It is this person who has lived in the apartment."

"I see," I said. "But I don't see what you're getting at."

"Julian," he said, "lived in this cesspool and I suppose Juju as well when they were on cordial terms if that was possible. I do not know... I would say no."

"So?"

"She returned to this place after you had the accident with Julian in the rest room. To go through the place and his belongings—only the lord could have cared what they were. She went back here I imagine tearing the place apart to find the money—"

"What money?"

"The money she took from Vermond. I should say which *Julian* took—blackmailing, I imagine, his own half-sister..."

"What're you talking about 'blackmailing'?" I asked.

Marlet was enjoying his salad as much as taunting me with his information. He had the dressing on his mustache and he bunched up the napkin to wipe his mouth.

"Oh, Jake," he said, with a weary sigh. "It is sad to rummage into all of this, but I am afraid I must if I'm to do my job in a reasonable manner, and to sleep nights with some idea that I did well..." He buttered a piece of bread carefully, and doctored it

177

heavily with mustard. I looked at my watch, and then he said, "The death of Vermond is the real question in all of this. We would like to close this case. Oh, the girl's murder matters a great deal, but as in all things, there must be distinctions, even in murder cases. But personally I would like some corroboration that Vermond's death was not a suicide. An intentional suicide is quite out of the picture—nor, Jake," he said quickly, "do I believe that his death was the result of a homicide."

"What then?" I said, "an accidental hanging?"

He smiled. "Yes—in a way, yes. I am not saying I have not discovered such deaths as Vermond's to be accidental, even with the deceased being hanged—sus*pended,* you see, hanging. Yes. These too have been accidental. Unfortunate. There is always some indication that the deceased intended to *not* be deceased, you understand. Some means at hand to free one's self from the actuality of hanging or strangling to *death.*"

"What are you saying," I asked. "Vermond wasn't instrumental in hanging himself?"

Marlet said, "The artist was dead before he was *hanged.*"

"Explaining the different sets of marks on his neck," I said.

He nodded. "He was hanged to give the appearance of a suicide. This is personal, Mr. Morgan—or Jake—"

"Yes, Jake's fine."

"So now I must ask perhaps an embarrassing question, and it is because of this that I asked to meet you informally."

"Okay," I said.

"In your relationship with Juju—and I am only curious, mind you, did you practice some form of..." He stopped and moved two fingers across his mouth. "What it is called—this asphyxia? Suffocation? Strangulation?"

I just stared at him. He nodded again, more slowly.

"I think you know what I am trying to say...? Being such a talented writer, you perhaps have a better word for it?" He was looking at my neck. I wondered if the bruises still showed. "Of course," he went on, "the outcome in Vermond's case *was* accidental—that is what I am convinced of."

I nodded. "You're saying he was strangled—but accidentally. Then he was strung up to appear that he'd done it himself?"

"Exactly," Marlet said. "You know exactly what I am thinking."

"So asphyxia's part of the scene," I said. "Vermond was into choking himself to get off."

"I suppose that too," he said, "or with the help of another. Naturally, what's done in one's privacy is one's own business."

"Naturally," I said.

"Unless it involves a danger to another person," he said. "A *serious* danger—"

"Like dying," I said.

"Like someone dying," he said. "Yes. It has been reported that Vermond had—how shall we say, unusual interests and avenues of personal satisfaction? He employed some form of asphyxia while he was engaged in a sexual activity—"

"With the girl—with Juju?"

Marlet nodded, sighing. "She was not the only one. There were others.... Juju was the most recent 'model', you might call her. That's what Vermond called them. As far as Juju is concerned, the proof is incontestible. We have recovered photographs that Vermond took of himself and Juju—time exposures—and there are ten-minutes on a video tape of a situation between them. Vermond and the girl."

"Where did you get these photographs?" I asked.

"One of Vermond's secret hiding places. It was necessary to take everything completely apart. They missed a great deal of money which he had inserted into the holes in the back of one of those old radios—a Firestone Air Chief from the mid-nineteen-thirties. He had a mass of large-denomination francs rolled into little tubes no bigger than match sticks, which he had inserted into the plug holes for the old tubes. Isn't that amazing?"

"When you say 'they' missed the money—"

"I mean the girl—and Julian. I imagine she explored in great depth that indoor, make-believe world of Vermond's."

"What happens on the video tape?" I asked.

"It depicts what I have described and establishes what I've suspected for some time."

"That he didn't kill himself..." I said.

"But that he died at the hands of the girl," he said. "At Juju's hands, Jake. I am convinced there was no intention of ever doing him serious harm." I asked if I could view the tape and he said, "No. It is a legal matter now with the estate. But I will tell you Vermond is lying on the chaise in a backwards manner, with his feet uplifted at the top of the chaise and with his head partly off the bottom edge—" He stopped.

"Go on," I said.

"Juju is tightening a rope around his neck. She is astride his torso and engaged in intercourse." He paused to drink water. "This few minute segment has been recorded into the middle of another tape—Vermond at a gallery. The tape is blank at the start. I have no idea if there was more than what we have. The rest of the tape goes back to the gallery—a showing. There is blank tape again, and there is nothing else on the remainder of this tape..."

I drank and watched him polish off the rest of the bread. He ate greedily, making sounds between bites. "So," I said, "what you're telling me is Juju killed Vermond—accidentally—"

"Yes," he said.

"In the heat of sex—" I started to say.

"Understand it takes but a moment—a second or so for the lack of oxygen to affect the brain—"

"Very well. The brother appears—"

"Oh, she has no doubt brought him in, Jake. Believing Vermond to have died at her hands—which *is* the case, whether we like it or not, but as an accident. I venture the idea was to dispose of the body, but I am sure for Julian it seemed opportunity was knocking upon his door. Together—or one assisting the other or visa versa, they tried to arrange a suicide scene. Most unsuccessfully. It was always apparent that he had not hanged himself. He had died as a result of strangulation, but at whose hands? Or had it been on his own? No... Sadly, the evidence is quite clear and yet none of this can be supported. So the mystery surrounding Vermond's death will remain neither fish nor foul, neither murder or suicide. Even if the girl had told you about it, it would remain hearsay now. It will stay a puzzle though I believe you and I know the answers. At least I do, my friend... All we have to do now, is close up this other matter—"

"The girl's death," I said.

It was like a cheesecloth shroud.

She was covered with it like a mummy and lying in a tray used for cremations without caskets or containers, and with a rim around the edges about four inches high. The tray was lowered on a kind of large paddle or spatula for pizzas, and mechanically inserted feet first into the oven—or retort, a small gray, firebrick-lined chamber that seemed flooded with light.

Pinaud had said, "Are you positive that you care to view the cremation, Mr. Morgan?" I said I was. In a moment, her cloth covered feet seem to burst into long twirling funnels of flame shooting upwards. There was no smoke. Instantly the cloth covering her burst into a sheet of fire, revealing her naked body which seemed to blister, the flesh and hair scorching.

Her skin singed, charred and burned. One hand came upwards slightly as if reaching out. It stayed rigid as the muscles contracted. Her thighs seemed to spread apart—a gradual widening and flexing of the limbs. Moments later the blackening skin of her stomach seemed to flutter or vibrate slightly, then the muscles split open in a kind of small explosion, the tissue charring quickly. The soft tissue seemed to wither, blackened and dissolve before my eyes, gradually exposing part of her skeleton. Her face had turned to a black covering which then broke into many charcoal like fragments, and quickly I was looking at her skull, and then the bones of the arms and legs appeared, starting at the fingers and feet and laying bare towards her torso.

Juju's ribs began to show while the hands and feet fell away from the larger bones, the little bones of her fingers, her wrists and ankles staying together for a surprisingly long time.

I jumped slightly as Pinaud placed a hand on my shoulder. He didn't say anything, but then as I took a step forward, his touch left and he turned away.

Alone, I watched as the girl's organs and contents of her abdomen burned slowly, the lungs even more slowly still. Her brain seemed resistant to catching on fire. I felt as though I was witness to some rite I couldn't have imagined.

But soon the insides of her body cavity disappeared and her spine became visible. In minutes, what remained of her intact skeleton fell apart like the walls and rafters of a collapsing barn. The bones glowed whitely in the flames.

The cremation took less than an hour.

The grayish white ash, spotted with yellowed bone fragments, was removed from the oven. Escorting me back into the mortuary, Pinaud explained that because the "cremains" often contained recognizable bone fragments, it was customary to "pulverize the cremains," and since I'd expressed a desire to scatter the ashes. He said the electric processor would grind the residual bone fragments to the size of sugar crystals.

In an anteroom off Pinaud's office, I found myself waiting in a mini-gallery surrounded with several Jean Paul Vermond paintings. Small glowing works of intense color—a countryside, a woman pouring milk from a bucket, a bald brown hillside with a cross sticking into it like a hat pin. A lonely stretch of road overhung with thick branches through which a vivid red sky seemed to radiate like the light of an explosion. They were all earlier paintings from several years before.

"I've collected Jean Paul's work since he attended the Beaux Arts," Pinaud said from the doorway. "I too was a student—a different branch of the arts."

"There's an odd sense of peace to these," I said. "A completeness and yet—there's a haunted kind of quality. They're quite remarkable."

Pinaud gazed past me to the stretch of road painting. "Jean

Paul walked with a shadow..."

He cleared his throat.

Escorting me to his office, Pinaud said, "There is no charge for the service, Mr. Morgan."

"I insist," I said. "I made the arrangements—"

"No, sir," he said. "There is absolutely no charge. I have done this for Jean Paul..." He turned and stared at me for a moment. "And for you."

Juju's ashes were in a cardboard container like an upended shoe box. He gently lifted the box and placed it into a paper sack. He stepped back, nodded, and said, "Go with god."

With the box cradled to my side, I walked from the mortuary south on Avenue George V and kept walking to where Avenue Montaigne intersected at Place de L'alma. Long, thin, pink and blue clouds had formed across the sky like streamers and I thought of Juju's toilet paper commercial—those long trails of light tissue sailing behind her.

The air had turned almost crisp. A kind of self-perpetuating sense kept me walking. There were no policemen in the shade and no one following me. There was no one. Soon I crossed the bridge onto the Left Bank and walked east along Quai D'Orsay. I kept walking and the picture of Juju throwing leaves into the air and her beaming face laughing through them stayed before me. I could almost hear her. I stopped at the edge of the Seine and listened to the water. The river looked dark. I opened the sack and brought out the box, opened it and the slight breeze gathered the fine powder from the top and blew it about like smoke.

Reaching out over the water, I turned the container upside down and the weight of the contents fell into the air, breaking apart into clouds.

Clusters of ash fell to the water while the powder swilled about, blowing over the surface. Some of the ash tunneled into the wind and the rest drifted a ways before going down into the river.

She was gone.

I worked all night and early the next morning two detectives I hadn't seen before came into the hotel. One waited in the lobby at the desk while the other, a chunky, large man, came to my door on the second floor. I wasn't dressed and asked him to wait in the hall. "Please leave the door ajar," he asked.

I was still dressing when he pushed the door open the rest of the way and said, "Please, monsieur. Will you come with us now?"

"Am I under arrest?" I asked.

He said, "Inspector Marlet is waiting for you."

"Yes," I said. "But you haven't answered my question."

He didn't answer it. But in the car I sat by myself in the backseat, the two of them in the front.

Marlet had the opened leopard skin suitcase on his desk into which he was poking with a pencil. He looked up at me as I entered the office and said, "Sit down."

I didn't. "Thanks, but I'll stand," I said. "Am I under arrest?"

"I told you to sit down!" he said sharply, reached across the desk and pushed me backwards with his hand. I went into the chair, feeling the blunt hard ends of his fingers as if they'd embedded in my skin.

"I'm sitting," I said.

"Now, I am sorry," he said. "All of this has made me very annoyed. Very frustrated, my friend. I'm not in a mood for games." From his side of the suitcase, he picked up a clear plastic sack that contained my Luger. "Is this your gun?"

I looked at it carefully. "Yes," I said. "It's quite valuable—"

"And very deadly," he said. "

"Where did you find it?" I asked. "Did you find it in the suitcase?"

"No," he said. "*I* did not find it in the suitcase—"

I said, "You've got it all wrong, Marlet, if you're trying to pin the girl's death on me—you've simply got it wrong."

"No, I am not wrong," he said. "I'm never wrong, Monsieur

Morgan. It is *you* who are wrong. You are not accused of anything now but somehow you are all tied into these events like a bad weed that has twisted through the body of something—"

"That's all very poetic," I said. "Perhaps you can get to the point—"

He threw my passport across the desk. I glared at him then snatched it up—flipped through it as Marlet drew in a deep breath and let it out slowly.

"The Iranian boy was picked up in Pigalle—" He gestured to the suitcase. "Your gun was in the valise. Was the magazine—the clip full when you last saw this gun?"

"No," I said. "There were five shells in the clip, but it wasn't in the gun. I only had five shells. They were all in the box—the original box the gun came in. The Iranian boy—"

"Tanyous," he said. "The other boy friend—"

"Oh..." I said. "I don't understand..."

"There are two shells in the gun now," Marlet said. "Three were ejected—the three spent cartridges that you could have spotted in the photograph of the scene I tried to show you." He sat down. "The Iranian's hand was covered with powder and he confessed to killing the girl."

"He confessed—Tanyous killed her?"

"Yes."

"I'm sorry," I said.

"Are you?"

"Yes. I'm very sorry all of this has happened."

"I am too," Marlet said. "The boy found her in that miserable hovel frequented by Julian—rented by the degenerate who is a homosexual. It seems Juju was searching the place. She had removed drawers and emptied cabinets. I assume looking for money, no doubt—whatever of Vermond's money Julian had hidden in that pig hole. Tanyous has admitted killing her. He admits finding the gun lying in the valise on the table in the kitchen. He says he fired three shots." I didn't say anything. "He has asked to see you."

"Me? Why?"

Marlet shrugged. "It is up to you if you want to see him. He is being transferred to a psychiatric ward this morning. You do not have to see him."

"I'll see him," I said and got to my feet. I held up the passport. "I gather I am free to go? You have no more suspicions to hurl at me?"

"Without the gun," he said, coming around the desk. "The weapon must remain. For a time." I followed him out of the office into the hall. As we went down some stairs, he said, "I am curious, *Jake*, to know what you feel?"

I looked at him. "Is this an official request?"

"No," he said. "But it is professional. One professional to another."

I said I wasn't sure what I felt. "What's going to happen to Tanyous?" I asked.

"He could be deported. No doubt we'll put him away here and if he behaves and doesn't get himself killed, he will probably be released or deported in the near future. None of that is up to me."

"Of course," I said. "Where is he?"

"We are almost there. He is downstairs in a holding cell." As we walked, Marlet said, "I once had the great pleasure of meeting Orson Welles in Paris. It was years ago. Such a great man. I remember his movie called *Lady from Shanghai* and I am now reminded of the scene where he describes people he is associating with as sharks feeding upon one another. What has happened reminds me of that scene and what he was describing..."

"It only seems profound to you, Inspector, from a selective point of view. Welles was actually describing the human condition from which neither you nor I can easily escape."

Smiling, Marlet brought us to a stop before a metal door. He rang a buzzer and looked through a glass porthole-like window, then looked at me. He had an almost pitying expression. Through the glass I saw a uniformed officer and the door was opened. Marlet asked the officer to take me to Tanyous, the Iranian.

The metal door shut behind me, locking electrically. The guard kept repeating, "Tanyous the Iranian—Tanyous..." Our footsteps echoed loudly on the concrete. He then asked, "Are you his counsel?" I said no.

A turn to the right and there he was—standing against the bars of an intersecting set of walls. It was a very small cell with an iron cot and a mattress.

Seeing me, he seemed to get excited and said, "Give me a cigarette! Please—have you got one?"

"You can keep the pack," I said, handing them through the bars. His face looked sick and weak, eyes sunken. His mouth pulled tight as he jammed a cigarette between his lips and quickly lit it. Breathing in the smoke deeply, he said, "I am glad he let you come down to see me. I told them that I killed Juju."

"Did you do it?" I asked.

He nodded, his eyes fixed on mine through the smoke. He'd been struck on the forehead and cheekbone. "You told them willingly?" I asked.

"Yes," he said. "I have you to thank for this. If you had not saved my life I wouldn't have lived to do it—" he laughed slightly. He was shaking. "It is so funny, isn't it? You and I—you killed him and I killed her—"

"I had to kill," I said. "He would've shot me again."

"Yes..." He inhaled more smoke, coughed, seemed to shake as if chilled. "It is ridiculous. I am ridiculous—I did not think it would be me who did this. Do you know what I am saying, Mr. Morgan?"

"Call me, Jake, please—"

"Yes, it is time to be less formal. I am saying I did not know that I was capable of doing something like I have done—except for being crazy."

"Are you?" I asked.

"I was crazy with her," he said. "I could not have done such a thing if I was not crazy. It was her. She had this..." He stopped.

"Is that going to be your defense? That you were crazy?" I asked.

"What defense can I offer for killing Juju—" he shrugged. A gesture very similar to Juju's. "It doesn't matter. I could have escaped out of France. But it does not matter. I am guilty and I have confessed to it. I would have killed myself if I had not confessed. That's why I took the gun with me—the Inspector wanted to know why I carried it away... To be caught with it? I said no, it was to kill myself. I had to find the place to kill myself but I turned out to be a coward even to myself."

I took a step closer, my face almost touching the pungent smelling steel of the bars separating us. It had a machine oil smell. "Why did you kill her?"

"She was leaving with Al—my closest friend. She was going to Germany. She stole my mother's ring—her and Al. They sold it for money to go to Germany." He sighed. "And I killed her because of you."

"What did I have to do with it?" I asked.

He was silent for several moments, intent on smoking. "Juju was a beautiful moth. A beautiful creature—but she carried a plague. She had an evil moving in her—it was like an aura. And she had a way—poor girl—some indirect way of drawing another into this aura—into this situation. With her, I—one—was in some kind of vacuum and the worst in one was brought out..."

I didn't say anything, just kept looking at him, watching him. Looking at his mouth and imagining her tongue going into it as it had in mine, her arms around him, his body pressing into hers. I had not owned her.

"It was almost as though one was brought into a situation with her in order to become a flame—she could set on fire, but it would be this same flame that would ruin her." He looked at me sadly. "It was only a matter of time before somebody killed her." He smiled slightly, nodding. "And here I am. Juju's fool. Like the American song. So that is me—Juju's fool."

"What will they do to you?" I asked.

Shrugging again, he said, "The Inspector says I will be sent for an evaluation by the doctors. Based on what develops with the doctors, they will prepare to prosecute me, I imagine. I was crazy at the time that this happened. It is honestly like I am watching someone else do it—but maybe that is a natural thing to feel—

when you are looking back at the terrible things. It is the truth. It is not something I am making up. Surely, Mr. Morgan, you must have had some moments with her when you believed you were losing some control over your emotions—even your mind?"

I was looking into his eyes and I saw that he knew the answer better than I. "Tanyous," I said, "I want you to tell me—if you can... I guess I am concerned that she didn't have much pain...?"

He was shaking his head. "The actual incident—it's a haze over. I remember the stairs in that awful place—horrible. Rats living in the walls and black people sleeping on the stairs—crawling over one another. I had to find the flat which was on the second floor in the back. I could see a window because the door was open part ways. This door—the paint and dirt was like scales on a dead fish... I opened it with my foot because I couldn't touch it. There were newspapers and cans—this Julian went in garbage piles and brought cans and junk into this flat, and everything was thrown around like it had been burglarized, but it had not, you see, because she was throwing things out of drawers. It was clothes—it was rags—I don't know what it was. Votive candles and there were pictures of Jesus everywhere. Stuck to the walls, Mr. Morgan. Cut out of newspapers and magazines and everywhere I imagine, and glued on the walls or put on with tape—with tacks. Everywhere was Jesus Christ—" Tanyous made a face and he started gasping as if breathless.

"Are you all right?" I asked.

He pulled out another cigarette with hands shaking so bad I had to light the match for him. "She did not even see me—bending over, yes. Her back was to me and she was behind the table at these cabinets. There was a suitcase opened on the table and I saw her underpants—the pink underpants, and other clothes and the gun was on top of a dress or some black underwear. When I picked it up she turned around and her eyes were right on me as I pointed the gun at her and pulled the trigger."

He took several quick puffs, blowing out the smoke. "It was like that... I don't even know why I did it except that it was in my hand and I had to. There was no choice. I do not understand—I've tried and tried but I can't understand. I didn't even talk to her. Didn't even say anything to her...

"The bullet hit her in the neck and she fell down like her legs were knocked out from under her by a train. She just seemed to lift up and fall down. She was on the floor holding her neck and the blood was coming out. I held the gun up a little and pulled the trigger again. This second shot was fired at the back of her head. And I shot her again—in the back somewhere." He took a deep drag on the cigarette, pulling the smoke deeply into his lungs. "So she did not feel any pain for very long."

He sighed and felt for a piece of tobacco on his lip. "I had the gun in the suitcase. I could not leave it behind though I did think of jumping off the roof or throwing myself in front of the Metro train. The police keep asking me about money and I do not know anything about money. I did not see any money and I did not think about money. I did wonder if anyone heard the shots. Strange, I do not remember leaving the building. But the gun—that was quick. And I couldn't use it. When it was taken away from me I felt as though I had already died. Do you understand what that feeling is like? I was dead but I was awake. I think I was dead from the moment I was standing over her in that awful place. She was so small on the dirty floor. So small... The poor moth girl..."

I was standing in the lobby at about the same place where Juju'd skated into me that first day. David was smiling as he handed me a wrapped present. "It is the best saki, Jake. Even in Japan it is the best saki. Very old, Jake. This is what the samurai drinks. You must open it in Tokyo."

"Thank you," I said. "I'm sorry you won't be helping me with this one."

"I will be home at Christmas, Jake. We will drink more saki then. But this is for you, and for Hiromi Nakasha to celebrate."

I tucked the saki carefully into my carryon just as a taxi

stopped in front of the hotel. Hiromi got out of the cab and hurried into the lobby in the same twelve-hundred dollar boots.

"Jake!" she said. "Do you have everything that is ready to go?"

"Yes," I said. "Everything's right here. I have two bags."

"Then we must hurry!" she said, beaming brightly. She looked wonderful. "We are taking an earlier flight and very soon we will be in Japan!"

Shouldering one bag and carrying the other, I said, "Okay. We can drink the saki on the plane." The driver was at the door, took the baggage and placed it in the trunk of the car. "Things have been unusual these days," I said. "I worked on the script all night."

Hiromi brushed her hair back with her hand. Her eyes were as black and shiny as wet olives. She leaned over and kissed me. I looked surprised. "I have wanted to kiss you since we met," she said. "Now I have kissed you, and we will be working very closely together in Tokyo. We will arrive before the sun sets. It is a wondrous light on the ocean, shining like a million tiny pieces of an endless mirror that has broken apart. It is a golden fire!"

Born and raised in Los Angeles, JOHN GILMORE has travelled the road to Fame in many guises: child actor, stage and motion picture player, poet, screenwriter, B-movie film director, journalist, true-crime writer and novelist. He has headed the writing program at Antioch University, and has taught and lectured extensively. Having made an indelible mark in investigative journalism *(Maximum Rock N Roll:* "John Gilmore is one of the best non-fiction writers of our time"), he is now focusing on novels and a second book of memoirs.

photo credit: Maike Paul Berlin